Python for Automated Trading Systems

Building Your Own Bots for Stock and Crypto Markets

J.P.Morgan

2

Discover Other Books in the Series

"Python for Algorithmic Trading: Mastering
Strategies for Consistent Profits"

"Python for Cryptocurrency Trading: Navigate the
Digital Currency Market"

"Python for Financial Data Analysis: Unlock the
Secrets of the Market"

"Python for Predictive Analytics in Finance:
Anticipate Market Movements"

Disclaimer

The content provided in this book, *Python for Automated Trading Systems: Building Your Own Bots for Stock and Crypto Markets*, by **J.P. Morgan**, is intended for educational and informational purposes only.

While the author has made every effort to ensure the accuracy and completeness of the information presented, no warranty or guarantee is given regarding the results or outcomes that may be obtained from using this information.

The author and publisher disclaim any liability for any direct, indirect, incidental, or consequential damages arising from the use of the information contained in this book.

Welcome to the privileged world of Trading Hackers!!!

Introduction

Welcome to *"**Python for Automated Trading Systems: Building Your Own Bots for Stock and Crypto Markets**."* If you're a web developer, Python programmer, web application developer, or student eager to harness the power of automation in the dynamic world of finance, you're in the right place.

In today's fast-paced financial landscape, the ability to react swiftly to market movements can make the difference between profit and loss. This is where automated trading systems come into play. By leveraging the power of Python, you can develop sophisticated trading bots that operate around the clock, executing trades with precision, speed, and consistency.

This book is your comprehensive guide to mastering the art and science of automated trading. Whether you're targeting the traditional stock markets or the rapidly evolving cryptocurrency space, the principles and techniques covered here will provide you with the tools and knowledge to create and optimize your own automated trading systems.

We'll start by laying a solid foundation, exploring the fundamentals of automated trading and the essential Python libraries you'll need. As we progress, you'll dive into data analysis, back testing strategies, and the intricacies of integrating with various trading platforms. You'll learn how to harness machine learning algorithms to predict market trends, implement robust risk management techniques, and even build high-frequency trading systems.

Chapter 1: Automated Trading Systems with Python

In recent years, the financial markets have seen a significant increase in the use of automated trading systems.These systems, also known as algorithmic trading or black-box trading, use computer algorithms to execute trades in the market without the need for human intervention. This has led to a more efficient and streamlinedtrading process, as well as increased liquidity and reduced transaction costs.

One of the most popular programming languages used for developing automated trading systems is Python. Python is a versatile and easy-to-learn language that is widely used in the financial industry for its simplicity andflexibility. In this chapter, we will introduce you to the basics of automated trading systems and how Python canbe used to create your own trading algorithms.

Automated trading systems work by analyzing market data, such as price movements and volume, and making decisions on when to buy or sell assets based on predefined rules. These rules can be as simple as buying when acertain moving average crosses above another moving average, or as complex as using machine learning algorithms to predict future price movements.

Python is an ideal language for developing automated trading systems because of its simplicity and readability. Python's syntax is easy to understand, making it easier for traders to write and debug their algorithms.

Additionally, Python has a wide range of libraries and tools that can be used to analyze market data and execute trades, such as pandas for data manipulation, matplotlib for data visualization, and the popular backtesting library backtrader.

To get started with automated trading systems in Python, you will need to install the necessary libraries and tools. The most important library for trading in Python is the Interactive Brokers API, which allows you to connect to your brokerage account and execute trades programmatically. You will also need to install pandas, numpy, and matplotlib for data analysis and visualization, as well as backtrader for backtesting your trading strategies.

Once you have installed the necessary libraries and tools, you can start developing your trading algorithms in Python. The first step is to define your trading strategy, which includes the rules for when to buy or sell assets based on market data. This can be done using simple if-else statements or more complex machine learning algorithms, depending on your level of expertise.

After defining your trading strategy, you can start backtesting it using historical market data. Backtesting is the process of testing your trading algorithm against past market data to see how well it would have performed in the past. This allows you to optimize your strategy and make any necessary adjustments before deploying it in a live trading environment.

Once you are satisfied with the performance of your trading algorithm in backtesting, you can start paper tradingor trading with real money in a live environment. Paper trading is the process of executing trades in a simulated environment without risking real money, allowing you to test your algorithm in real-time market conditions.

Automated trading systems have revolutionized the financial markets by making trading more efficient and reducing human error. Python is an ideal language for developing automated trading systems because of its simplicity and flexibility.

By following the steps outlined in this chapter, you can start developingyour own automated trading algorithms in Python and take advantage of the opportunities in the financial markets.

Evolution of Trading Systems with python

Trading systems have evolved significantly over the years, with advancements in technology playing a key role in shaping the way trades are executed. One of the most popular programming languages used in the development of trading systems is Python. Python is a versatile and powerful language that is widely used in the financial industry for its simplicity, flexibility, and ease of use.

Python has become the language of choice for many traders and developers due to its extensive libraries and tools that make it easy to implement complex trading strategies. In this article, we will explore the evolution of trading systems with Python and how it has revolutionized the way trades are conducted.

The Evolution of Trading Systems

Trading systems have come a long way since the early days of open outcry trading on the trading floors of stock exchanges. In the past, traders would physically buy and sell securities by shouting out their orders to brokers on the trading floor. This manual method of trading was slow, inefficient, and prone to human error.

With the advent of electronic trading platforms in the 1980s, trading systems began to shift towards automation. Electronic trading platforms allowed traders to execute trades electronically, without the need for human intervention. This led to faster execution times, increased liquidity, and reduced trading costs.

As technology continued to advance, trading systems became more sophisticated and complex. High-frequency trading (HFT) emerged as a new form of trading that relied on algorithmic strategies to execute trades at lightning speed. HFT firms used powerful computers and advanced algorithms to analyze market data and execute trades in milliseconds.

The rise of algorithmic trading paved the way for the development of automated trading systems. These systems use pre-defined rules and algorithms to execute trades automatically based on market conditions. Automated trading systems can execute trades faster and more efficiently than human traders, leading to increased profits and reduced risk.

Python and Trading Systems

Python has become the language of choice for many traders and developers due to its simplicity, flexibility, and ease of use. Python is an open-source programming language that is widely used in the financial industry for its extensive libraries and tools that make it easy to implement complex trading strategies.

One of the main reasons why Python is so popular in the development of trading systems is its extensive libraries for data analysis and visualization. Libraries such as NumPy, pandas, and matplotlib make it easy to manipulate and analyze large datasets, allowing traders to make informed decisions based on data-driven insights.

Python also has a wide range of libraries for machine learning and artificial intelligence, which can be used to develop predictive models for trading. Machine learning algorithms can analyze historical market data and identify patterns and trends that can be used to predict future price movements.

Another advantage of Python is its simplicity and readability. Python code is easy to read and understand, making it ideal for traders and developers who may not have a background in programming. Python's syntax is clean and concise, making it easy to write and debug code quickly.

Python also has a large and active community of developers who contribute to the development of libraries and tools for trading. This community-driven approach has led to the creation of a wide range of open-source libraries and frameworks that can be used to build trading systems quickly and efficiently.

Python in Action: Building a Trading System

To illustrate how Python can be used to build a trading system, let's walk through a simple example of a moving average crossover strategy. This strategy involves using two moving averages - a short-term moving average and a long-term moving average - to generate buy and sell signals.

First, we need to import the necessary libraries for data analysis and visualization:

```python
```

```
import numpy as npimport pandas as pd
import matplotlib.pyplot as plt
```

Next, we need to load historical price data for a stock using the pandas library:

```python
data = pd.read_csv('stock_data.csv')
```

We can then calculate the short-term and long-term moving averages using the rolling() function in pandas:

```python
data['short_ma']                                        =
data['close'].rolling(window=20).mean() data['long_ma'] =
data['close'].rolling(window=50).mean()
```

Next, we can generate buy and sell signals based on the moving average crossover strategy:

```python
data['signal']        =        np.where(data['short_ma']        >
data['long_ma'], 1, 0)data['position'] = data['signal'].diff()
```

Finally, we can plot the stock price data along with the moving averages and buy and sell signals:

```python plt.figure(figsize=(12, 6))
plt.plot(data['close'],               label='Close               Price')
```

16

```
plt.plot(data['short_ma'],           label='Short           MA')
plt.plot(data['long_ma'], label='Long MA')

plt.plot(data[data['position']           ==           1].index,
data['short_ma'][data['position']           ==           1],           '^',
markersize=10, color='g',lw=0, label='Buy Signal')
plt.plot(data[data['position
```

Importance of Automation in Trading

Automation in trading refers to the use of computer programs and algorithms to automatically execute trades in the financial markets. This technology has revolutionized the way trades are conducted, making them faster, more efficient, and less prone to human error. In recent years, automation has become increasingly popular among traders and investors, as it offers a number of significant advantages over manual trading.

One of the key benefits of automation in trading is the ability to execute trades at lightning speed. Computers can process information and make decisions much faster than humans, allowing automated trading systems to react to market changes in real-time. This speed is crucial in fast-paced markets where prices can fluctuate rapidly, as it enables traders to take advantage of opportunities before they disappear.

Another important advantage of automation in trading is the elimination of human emotions from the decision-making process. Emotions such as fear and greed can cloud judgment and lead to irrational trading decisions, resulting in losses. Automated trading systems follow pre-defined rules and algorithms, which are not influenced by emotions, ensuring that trades are executed based on objective criteria rather than gut feelings.

Automation also allows traders to backtest their strategies on historical data before deploying them in live markets. This enables traders to evaluate the performance of their strategies and make any necessary adjustments before risking real capital. Backtesting can help traders identify weaknesses in their strategies and optimize them for better results, leading to more consistent and profitable trading.

In addition, automation in trading can help traders manage risk more effectively. Automated systems can incorporate risk management techniques such as stop-loss orders and position sizing rules to protect capital and minimize losses. These risk management tools are executed automatically, reducing the likelihood of human error and ensuring that trades are managed in a disciplined manner.

Automation in trading also offers the advantage of scalability. Automated trading systems can handle large volumes of trades simultaneously, allowing traders to diversify their portfolios and take advantage of multiple opportunities across different markets. This scalability can help traders grow their accounts more quickly and efficiently than manual trading methods.

Furthermore, automation in trading can help traders overcome the limitations of human capacity. Humans have a limited ability to monitor multiple markets and assets simultaneously, which can result in missed opportunities or delayed reactions to market events. Automated trading systems can monitor multiple markets in real-time and execute trades across different assets simultaneously, enabling traders to capitalize on a wider range of opportunities.

Overall, automation in trading offers a number of

significant advantages, including speed, efficiency, emotion-free decision-making, backtesting capabilities, risk management tools, scalability, and the ability to overcome human limitations. These benefits have made automation an essential tool for traders and investors looking to stay competitive in today's fast-paced and complex financial markets.

Automation in trading is a powerful technology that has transformed the way trades are conducted in the financial markets. By leveraging the speed, efficiency, and objectivity of automated systems, traders can improve their trading performance, manage risk more effectively, and capitalize on a wider range of opportunities.

As technology continues to evolve, automation in trading is likely to become even more prevalent, offering traders new ways to enhance their trading strategies and achieve better results.

Chapter 2: Setting Up Your Python Environment

In order to start writing and running Python code, you need to set up your Python environment. This chapter will guide you through the process of installing Python on your computer, setting up a coding environment, and understanding the basics of Python programming.

Installing Python

The first step in setting up your Python environment is to install the Python interpreter on your computer. Python is an open-source programming language, which means that it is free to download and use. You can download the latest version of Python from the official Python website (www.python.org).

When downloading Python, make sure to select the appropriate version for your operating system. Python is available for Windows, macOS, and Linux. Once you have downloaded the installer, run it and follow the on-screen instructions to install Python on your computer.

Setting Up a Coding Environment

After installing Python, you will need a coding environment where you can write and run Python code. There are several options available for coding environments, including text editors, integrated development environments (IDEs), and online code editors.

One popular choice for a coding environment is Visual Studio Code, a free and open-source code editor developed by Microsoft. Visual Studio Code supports Python out of the box and provides features such as syntax highlighting, code completion, and debugging tools.

Another popular option is PyCharm, a powerful IDE developed by JetBrains. PyCharm offers advanced features for Python development, such as intelligent code completion, refactoring tools, and unit testing support.

If you prefer a simpler coding environment, you can use online code editors such as Repl.it or Jupyter Notebook. These online editors allow you to write and run Python code directly in your web browser, without the need to install any software on your computer.

Understanding Python Basics

Once you have set up your Python environment, it is time to start learning the basics of Python programming. Python is a versatile and easy-to-learn programming language that is widely used in various fields, such as web development, data analysis, and artificial intelligence.

One of the key features of Python is its readability. Python code is easy to read and understand, thanks to its simple syntax and indentation-based structure. This makes Python a great language for beginners who are just starting to learn programming.

In Python, you can use variables to store data, such as numbers, strings, and lists. Variables are assigned using the
= operator, and their values can be changed throughout the program. For example, you can create a variable called x and assign it the value 10: x = 10

You can also use built-in functions in Python to perform common tasks, such as printing output to the console, reading input from the user, and performing mathematical operations. For example, you can use the print() function to display a message on the screen:

print("Hello, World!")

In addition to variables and functions, Python also supports control structures such as if statements, for loops, and while loops. These control structures allow you to make decisions and repeat actions based on certain conditions. For example, you can use an if statement to check if a number is greater than 10:

```
x = 15
if x > 10:
print("x is greater than 10")Conclusion
```
Setting up your Python environment is the first step towards becoming a proficient Python programmer. By installing Python, setting up a coding environment, and understanding the basics of Python programming, you will be well on your way to writing and running Python code.

In the next chapter, we will dive deeper into Python programming concepts, such as data types, functions, and modules. Stay tuned for more exciting Python tutorials!

Installing Necessary Libraries for Trading Systems with python

Python has become one of the most popular programming languages for developing trading systems due to its simplicity, versatility, and robustness. In order to build a successful trading system in Python, it is essential to install the necessary libraries that will provide the tools and functionalities needed for data analysis, strategy development, backtesting, and execution.

In this article, we will discuss the key libraries that are commonly used in trading systems and provide a step-by-step guide on how to install them in your Python environment.

NumPy: NumPy is a fundamental package for scientific computing in Python. It provides support for large, multi-dimensional arrays and matrices, along with a collection of mathematical functions to operate on these arrays. NumPy is essential for performing data manipulation and analysis in trading systems.

To install NumPy, you can use the following command in your terminal or command prompt:

```bash
pip install numpy
```

Pandas: Pandas is a powerful data manipulation and analysis library built on top of NumPy. It provides data structures like DataFrame and Series that make it easy to work with structured data. Pandas is widely used in trading systems for data preprocessing, cleaning, and analysis.

To install Pandas, you can use the following command:

```bash
pip install pandas
```

Matplotlib: Matplotlib is a plotting library for creating static, animated, and interactive visualizations in Python. It is commonly used in trading systems to visualize historical price data, performance metrics, and trading signals.

To install Matplotlib, you can use the following command:

```bash
pip install matplotlib
```

TA-Lib: TA-Lib is a technical analysis library for Python that provides over 150 indicators for analyzing financial data. These indicators can be used to develop trading strategies and generate trading signals based on technical analysis.

To install TA-Lib, you can download the source code from the official GitHub repository (https://github.com/mrjbq7/ta-lib) and follow the installation instructions provided in the README file.

Backtrader: Backtrader is a popular Python library for backtesting trading strategies. It provides a flexible and modular framework for designing, testing, and optimizing trading strategies using historical market data.

To install Backtrader, you can use the following command:

```bash
pip install backtrader
```

ccxt: ccxt is a cryptocurrency trading library that provides a unified API for connecting to various cryptocurrency exchanges. It allows traders to access market data, execute trades, and manage their portfolios across multiple exchanges.

To install ccxt, you can use the following command:

```bash
pip install ccxt
```

Alpaca Trade API: Alpaca is a commission-free trading platform that provides a RESTful API for accessing market data and executing trades. The Alpaca Trade API can be integrated into Python trading systems to automate trading strategies and manage portfolios.

To install the Alpaca Trade API, you can use the following command:

```bash
pip install alpaca-trade-api
```

TensorFlow: TensorFlow is an open-source machine learning library developed by Google for building and training deep learning models. It can be used in trading systems to develop predictive models for forecasting market trends and making trading decisions.

To install TensorFlow, you can use the following command:

```bash
pip install tensorflow
```

Keras: Keras is a high-level neural networks API built on top of TensorFlow that simplifies the process of building and training deep learning models. It provides a user-friendly interface for designing and testing neural networks in trading systems.

To install Keras, you can use the following command:

```bash
pip install keras
```

Scikit-learn: Scikit-learn is a machine learning library for

Python that provides a wide range of algorithms for classification, regression, clustering, and dimensionality reduction. It can be used in trading systems for building predictive models and optimizing trading strategies.

To install Scikit-learn, you can use the following command:

```bash
pip install scikit-learn
```

Installing the necessary libraries for trading systems in Python is essential for developing robust and efficient trading strategies. By following the steps outlined in this article, you can set up your Python environment with the key libraries needed for data analysis, strategy development, backtesting, and execution.

With the right tools and resources at your disposal, you can build successful trading systems that capitalize on market opportunities and maximize profits.

How to improve your python setup for trading system

Python is a powerful programming language that is widely used in the financial industry for developing trading systems. However, setting up a Python environment for trading can be a daunting task for beginners. In this article, we will discuss how you can improve your Python setup for trading systems to make your workflow more efficient and productive.

Use a Virtual Environment:

One of the best practices for setting up a Python environment for trading systems is to use a virtual environment.A virtual environment allows you to create an isolated environment for your project, which helps in managing dependencies and avoiding conflicts with other projects. You can create a virtual environment using the venv module, which is included in the Python standard library.

To create a virtual environment, open a terminal and run the following command:
```
python -m venv myenv
```

This will create a new virtual environment named `myenv` in the current directory. You can activate the virtual environment by running the following command:
```
```

```
source myenv/bin/activate
```
```

Once the virtual environment is activated, you can install the required packages for your trading system using pip. This will ensure that the dependencies are installed in the virtual environment and not globally on your system.

Use a Package Manager:
Managing dependencies for a trading system can be challenging, especially when you have multiple projects with different requirements. Using a package manager such as pipenv or poetry can help you manage dependencies more efficiently. These tools allow you to specify the dependencies for your project in a `Pipfile` or `pyproject.toml` file and automatically install them in the virtual environment.

To use pipenv, first install it using pip:
```
pip install pipenv
```
```

Next, navigate to your project directory and run the following command to create a new virtual environment and install the dependencies specified in the `Pipfile`:
```
pipenv install
```
```

This will create a new virtual environment and install the required packages for your trading system. You can then activate the virtual environment by running:
```

```
pipenv shell
```

Use Jupyter Notebooks for Analysis:
Jupyter Notebooks are a popular tool for data analysis and visualization in Python. You can use Jupyter Notebooks to analyze historical data, develop trading strategies, and visualize the performance of your trading system. Jupyter Notebooks allow you to write and execute Python code in an interactive environment, making it easier to explore and experiment with different ideas.

To install Jupyter Notebooks, you can use pip:
```
pip install jupyter
```

Once Jupyter Notebooks is installed, you can start a new notebook by running the following command:
```
jupyter notebook
```

This will open a new browser window with the Jupyter Notebook interface, where you can create a new notebook and start writing Python code. You can import libraries such as pandas, numpy, and matplotlib to analyze data and visualize the results of your trading system.

Use Version Control:

Version control is essential for managing the codebase of your trading system and collaborating with other developers. Using a version control system such as Git allows you to track changes, revert to previous versions, and work on different features in parallel. You can use platforms like GitHub or GitLab to host your code repository and collaborate with other developers.

To initialize a new Git repository for your trading system, navigate to your project directory and run the following command:
```
git init
```

This will create a new Git repository in the current directory. You can then add your files to the repository and commit your changes using the following commands:
```
git add .
git commit -m "Initial commit"
```

To push your code to a remote repository on GitHub, you can create a new repository on the platform and add it as a remote to your local repository:
```
git remote add origin
git push -u origin master
```

This will push your code to the remote repository on GitHub, where you can collaborate with other developers and track the changes to your trading system.

Use Automated Testing:
Automated testing is crucial for ensuring the reliability and performance of your trading system. Writing unit tests for your codebase allows you to catch bugs early, verify the correctness of your algorithms, and refactor code with confidence. You can use testing frameworks such as pytest or unittest to write and run tests for your trading system.

To install pytest, you can use pip:
```
pip install pytest
```

You can then write test cases for your trading system in separate Python files and run them using the pytest command:
```
pytest
```

This will run all the test cases in your project and report any failures or errors. You can use pytest fixtures to set up common test data and reuse them across multiple test cases, making your test suite more maintainable and efficient.

Chapter 3: Fundamentals of Automated Trading

Automated trading, also known as algorithmic trading, is a method of executing trades using computer algorithms. These algorithms are programmed to follow a set of predefined rules and criteria to make trading decisions without human intervention. Automated trading has become increasingly popular in the financial markets due to its ability to execute trades at high speeds and with precision.

In this chapter, we will explore the fundamentals of automated trading, including its benefits, risks, and key components. We will also discuss the different types of automated trading strategies and how they can be implemented in the financial markets.

Benefits of Automated Trading

One of the key benefits of automated trading is its ability to execute trades at high speeds. With automated trading, trades can be executed in a fraction of a second, allowing traders to take advantage of market opportunities as soon as they arise. This speed is crucial in fast-moving markets where prices can change rapidly.

Another benefit of automated trading is its ability to remove human emotions from trading decisions. Emotionssuch as fear and greed can often cloud judgment and lead to irrational trading decisions. By using computer algorithms to make trading decisions, traders can avoid these emotional biases and stick to their predefined trading rules.

Automated trading also allows for backtesting of trading strategies. Traders can test their strategies on historical data to see how they would have performed in the past. This allows traders to refine their strategies and make adjustments before deploying them in live trading.

Risks of Automated Trading

While automated trading offers many benefits, it also comes with its own set of risks. One of the main risks of automated trading is the potential for technical failures. If the trading algorithm malfunctions or encounters a technical issue, it can result in significant losses for the trader. It is important for traders to have safeguards in place to prevent and mitigate these technical failures.

Another risk of automated trading is over-optimization. Traders may be tempted to tweak their trading algorithms to perform well on historical data, but this can lead to overfitting. Overfitting occurs when a tradingstrategy is too closely tailored to historical data and performs poorly in live trading. Traders must strike a balance between optimizing their strategies and ensuring they are robust enough to perform well in real-world conditions.

Key Components of Automated Trading

There are several key components of automated trading that traders must understand in order to successfully implement automated trading strategies. These components include:

Trading platform: The trading platform is the software that allows traders to execute trades using their automated trading algorithms. There are many different trading platforms available, each with its own features and capabilities.

Data feed: The data feed provides traders with real-time market data, such as price quotes and volume information. This data is essential for making informed trading decisions and executing trades at the right time.

Trading strategy: The trading strategy is the set of rules and criteria that the automated trading algorithm follows to make trading decisions. Traders must carefully design and test their trading strategies to ensure they are profitable and robust.

Types of Automated Trading Strategies

There are several different types of automated trading strategies that traders can use to execute trades in the financial markets. Some common types of automated trading strategies include:

Trend-following strategies: Trend-following strategies aim to profit from the momentum of a particular asset.These strategies buy when the asset is trending upwards and sell when it is trending downwards.

Mean reversion strategies: Mean reversion strategies aim

to profit from the tendency of asset prices to revert to their average value over time. These strategies buy when the asset is undervalued and sell when it is overvalued.

Arbitrage strategies: Arbitrage strategies aim to profit from price discrepancies between different markets or assets. These strategies buy in one market and sell in another to capture the price difference.

In conclusion, automated trading is a powerful tool that can help traders execute trades at high speeds and with precision. By understanding the fundamentals of automated trading, including its benefits, risks, key components, and types of strategies, traders can effectively implement automated trading strategies in the financial markets. It is important for traders to carefully design and test their trading strategies to ensure they are profitable and robust in real-world conditions.

Key Market Finance Concepts

Finance is a crucial aspect of any business or economy, as it involves the management of money and other assets.In order to understand the world of finance, it is important to grasp some key market finance concepts. These concepts are fundamental to making informed decisions about investments, managing risk, and achieving financial goals. In this article, we will explore some of the key market finance concepts that are essential for anyone looking to navigate the complex world of finance.

One of the most important concepts in finance is the concept of risk and return. This concept states that the potential return on an investment is directly related to the level of risk associated with that investment. In general, investments with higher levels of risk have the potential for higher returns, while investments with lower levels of risk tend to have lower returns. Understanding this relationship is crucial for investors, as it allows them to make informed decisions about where to allocate their money.

Another important concept in finance is diversification. Diversification involves spreading investments across a variety of assets in order to reduce risk. By diversifying their investments, investors can protect themselves from the negative impact of a single asset performing poorly. Diversification is a key strategy for managing risk and achieving long-term financial success.

Asset allocation is another important concept in finance.

Asset allocation involves determining how to distribute investments across different asset classes, such as stocks, bonds, and real estate. By carefully allocating assets, investors can achieve a balance between risk and return that aligns with their financial goals and risk tolerance.

Market efficiency is another key concept in finance. Market efficiency refers to the idea that asset prices reflect all available information and that it is impossible to consistently outperform the market. This concept has important implications for investors, as it suggests that it is difficult to beat the market through stock picking or market timing. Understanding market efficiency can help investors make more informed decisions about their investment strategies.

Liquidity is another important concept in finance. Liquidity refers to the ease with which an asset can be bought or sold without significantly impacting its price. Assets that are highly liquid, such as stocks and bonds, are easier to buy and sell, while assets that are illiquid, such as real estate or private equity, may be more difficult to sell quickly. Understanding liquidity is important for investors, as it can impact their ability to access their money when needed.

Another important concept in finance is the time value of money. The time value of money states that a dollar received today is worth more than a dollar received in the future, due to the potential for that dollar to earn interest or be invested. This concept is crucial for understanding the impact of inflation and interest rates on the value of money over time.

One of the key concepts in finance is the concept of compounding. Compounding refers to the process of earning interest on both the initial investment and the accumulated interest. Over time, compounding can significantly increase the value of an investment, as the interest earned on the investment continues to grow. Understanding the power of compounding can help investors make smart decisions about saving and investing for the future.

Inflation is another important concept in finance. Inflation refers to the gradual increase in the price of goods and services over time. Inflation erodes the purchasing power of money, as the same amount of money buys fewer goods and services as prices rise. Understanding inflation is crucial for investors, as it can impact the real return on investments and the value of money over time.

Another key concept in finance is the concept of leverage. Leverage involves using borrowed money to increase the potential return on an investment. While leverage can amplify gains, it can also amplify losses, making it a risky strategy. Understanding the risks and rewards of leverage is important for investors, as it can impact their overall risk profile and financial stability.

Finally, the concept of financial markets is essential for understanding the world of finance. Financial markets are where buyers and sellers come together to trade financial assets such as stocks, bonds, and commodities.
These markets play a crucial role in allocating capital,

setting prices, and facilitating economic activity. Understanding how financial markets work can help investors make informed decisions about where to invest their money and how to navigate the complexities of the financial system.

Understanding key market finance concepts is essential for anyone looking to navigate the worldof finance. Concepts such as risk and return, diversification, asset allocation, market efficiency, liquidity, the time value of money, compounding, inflation, leverage, and financial markets are fundamental to making informed decisions about investments, managing risk, and achieving financial goals. By mastering these concepts, investors can build a solid foundation for long-term financial success.

Differences Between Stocks and Cryptocurrencies

Stocks and cryptocurrencies are two popular investment options that have gained significant attention in recent years. While both offer the potential for high returns, there are several key differences between the two that investors should be aware of before deciding where to put their money.

One of the main differences between stocks and cryptocurrencies is the underlying asset. Stocks represent ownership in a company, meaning that when you buy a stock, you are purchasing a small piece of that company. This entitles you to a share of the company's profits, as well as voting rights on important company decisions.

On the other hand, cryptocurrencies are digital assets that exist on a decentralized network, such as blockchain. They are not backed by any physical asset or company, but rather derive their value from supply and demand dynamics.

Another key difference between stocks and cryptocurrencies is the level of regulation. Stocks are heavily regulated by government agencies, such as the Securities and Exchange Commission (SEC), to ensure transparency and protect investors. Companies that issue stocks must adhere to strict reporting requirements and disclosure rules. Cryptocurrencies, on the other hand, operate in a largely unregulated environment. While some countries have implemented regulations to govern the use of cryptocurrencies, many are still in the process of developing a clear regulatory framework.

The volatility of stocks and cryptocurrencies is another important distinction. Stocks are generally considered to be less volatile than cryptocurrencies, as they are backed by tangible assets and are influenced by factors such as company performance, economic conditions, and market trends.

Cryptocurrencies, on the other hand, are known for their extreme price fluctuations, with values often swinging by double-digit percentages in a single day. This high volatility can be both a blessing and a curse for investors, as it offers the potential for quick profits but also carries a high level of risk.

Liquidity is another factor that sets stocks and cryptocurrencies apart. Stocks are traded on established stock exchanges, such as the New York Stock Exchange (NYSE) or the Nasdaq, which provide a high level of liquidityand ensure that investors can easily buy and sell shares at any time. Cryptocurrencies, on the other hand, are traded on various online platforms and exchanges, which may have lower liquidity levels and can make it more difficult to execute trades quickly, especially for less popular coins.

One of the biggest differences between stocks and cryptocurrencies is the level of access and inclusivity they offer to investors. Stocks have traditionally been the domain of institutional investors and wealthy individuals, asthey require a brokerage account and significant capital to invest. Cryptocurrencies, on the other hand, have democratized the investment landscape by allowing anyone with an internet connection to buy and trade digital assets. This has opened up the world of investing to a much broader audience, including retail investors and those in developing countries who may not have access to traditional financial markets.

The technology behind stocks and cryptocurrencies is also vastly different. Stocks are traded on traditional exchanges using centralized systems that are maintained by financial institutions and regulatory bodies.

Cryptocurrencies, on the other hand, are built on decentralized blockchain technology, which allows for peer-to- peer transactions without the need for intermediaries. This technology has the potential to revolutionize the way we think about money and finance, but it also comes with its own set of challenges, such as scalability and security concerns.

In terms of risk, both stocks and cryptocurrencies carry their own set of risks that investors should be aware of. Stocks are subject to market risks, such as economic downturns, industry disruptions, and company-specific factors that can impact the value of a stock. Cryptocurrencies, on the other hand, are exposed to unique risks, such as regulatory uncertainty, hacking attacks, and market manipulation. Investors should carefully consider their risk tolerance and investment goals before deciding to invest in either asset class.

Despite their differences, stocks and cryptocurrencies can both be valuable additions to a well-diversified investment portfolio. Stocks offer the potential for long-term growth and income through dividends, while cryptocurrencies provide the opportunity for high-risk, high-reward investments in a rapidly evolving market. By understanding the key differences between the two asset classes and conducting thorough research, investors can make informed decisions that align with their financial goals and risk tolerance.

Stocks and cryptocurrencies are two distinct investment options that offer unique benefits and risks. While stocks represent ownership in a company and are subject to strict regulations and market dynamics, cryptocurrencies are digital assets that operate on decentralized networks and are known for their high volatilityand potential for quick profits.

By understanding the differences between the two asset classes and conducting thorough research, investors can make informed decisions that align with their financial goals and risk tolerance.Ultimately, the decision to invest in stocks or cryptocurrencies will depend on individual preferences, investmentobjectives, and risk appetite.

Chapter 4: Introduction to Trading Algorithms

In the world of finance, trading algorithms have become an essential tool for investors looking to make informed decisions and maximize their profits. These algorithms are computer programs that use mathematical models and historical data to predict market trends and execute trades automatically. In this chapter, we will explore the basics of trading algorithms, how they work, and the different types of algorithms commonly used in the financial markets.

Trading algorithms are designed to analyze vast amounts of data in real-time and make split-second decisions based on predefined rules and parameters. These algorithms can be used to execute trades in a variety of financial instruments, including stocks, bonds, commodities, and currencies. By using algorithms, investors can take advantage of market opportunities and reduce the impact of human emotions on trading decisions.

There are several key components of a trading algorithm, including data collection, analysis, strategy formulation, and trade execution. Data collection involves gathering information from various sources, such as market prices, volume, and news feeds. This data is then analyzed using statistical models and algorithms to identify patterns and trends that can be used to predict future market movements.

Once the data has been analyzed, the algorithm

formulates a trading strategy based on predefined rules and parameters. These rules can be as simple as buying or selling a security based on a specific price movement or as complex as using machine learning algorithms to identify patterns in the data. The algorithm then executes trades automatically based on the strategy, taking into account factors such as risk tolerance, market conditions, and trading costs.

There are several types of trading algorithms commonly used in the financial markets, including trend-following algorithms, mean-reversion algorithms, and arbitrage algorithms. Trend-following algorithms aim to profit from the momentum of a security by buying when prices are rising and selling when prices are falling. Mean-reversion algorithms, on the other hand, aim to profit from the tendency of prices to revert to their historical averages by buying low and selling high.

Arbitrage algorithms seek to profit from price discrepancies between different markets or securities by buying in one market and selling in another. These algorithms are often used by high-frequency traders who capitalize on small price differences that occur in milliseconds. By using trading algorithms, investors can take advantage of market inefficiencies and generate consistent profits over time.

In addition to these types of algorithms, there are also algorithmic trading strategies that combine multiple algorithms to create a diversified portfolio. These strategies can be tailored to individual investors' risk tolerance, investment goals, and time horizons. By using a combination of algorithms, investors can reduce their exposure to market volatility and maximize their returns.

Overall, trading algorithms have revolutionized the way investors trade in the financial markets. By using sophisticated mathematical models and real-time data analysis, these algorithms can make informed decisions and execute trades faster and more efficiently than human traders. Whether you are a novice investor or an experienced trader, understanding how trading algorithms work can help you navigate the complex world of finance and achieve your investment goals.

Algorithmic Trading Strategy

Algorithmic trading is a method of executing trades using automated pre-programmed trading instructions accounting for variables such as time, price, and volume. This type of trading relies on complex algorithms to make decisions on when to buy or sell assets in the financial markets. Algorithmic trading has become increasingly popular in recent years due to its ability to execute trades at high speeds and frequencies, allowing traders to take advantage of market opportunities that may not be available to manual traders.

There are many different algorithmic trading strategies that traders can use to generate profits in the financial markets. One common strategy is trend-following, where algorithms are programmed to identify and follow trends in asset prices. These algorithms will buy assets when prices are rising and sell assets when prices are falling, in an attempt to capture profits from the trend. Another popular strategy is mean reversion, where algorithms are programmed to buy assets that are trading below their historical averages and sell assets that are trading above their historical averages, in an attempt to profit from price reversals.

One important aspect of algorithmic trading is risk management. Traders must carefully manage the risks associated with algorithmic trading to avoid significant losses. This can be done by setting stop-loss orders to limit potential losses, diversifying the portfolio to spread risk across different assets, and monitoring the performance of algorithms to identify and correct any issues that may arise.

Another key aspect of algorithmic trading is backtesting. Backtesting is the process of testing a trading strategy using historical data to see how it would have performed in the past. This allows traders to evaluate the effectiveness of their algorithms and make any necessary adjustments before deploying them in live trading.
Backtesting can help traders identify potential flaws in their strategies and optimize them for better performance.

In addition to trend-following and mean reversion strategies, there are many other algorithmic trading strategies that traders can use to generate profits in the financial markets. Some traders use arbitrage strategies, where algorithms are programmed to take advantage of price differences between different markets or assets. Other traders use momentum strategies, where algorithms are programmed to buy assets that are showing strong upward momentum and sell assets that are showing strong downward momentum.

One important consideration when developing an algorithmic trading strategy is the choice of programming language. There are many different programming languages that can be used to develop algorithmic trading strategies, but some of the most popular languages include Python, R, and C++. Each language has its own strengths and weaknesses, so traders should choose a language that best suits their needs and preferences.

Python is a popular programming language for algorithmic

trading due to its simplicity and flexibility. Python is easy to learn and has a large number of libraries and frameworks that can be used to develop algorithmic trading strategies. Python is also widely used in the financial industry, making it a popular choice among traders.

R is another popular programming language for algorithmic trading, particularly among statisticians and data scientists. R is well-suited for analyzing and visualizing data, making it a good choice for traders who want to incorporate data analysis into their trading strategies. R also has a large number of libraries and packages that can be used to develop algorithmic trading strategies.

C++ is a powerful programming language that is commonly used in high-frequency trading due to its speed and efficiency. C++ is a lower-level language compared to Python and R, but it offers greater control over hardware resources, making it ideal for high-frequency trading strategies that require fast execution speeds.

Algorithmic trading is a powerful tool that can help traders generate profits in the financial markets. By using complex algorithms to make trading decisions, traders can take advantage of market opportunities that may not be available to manual traders.

When developing an algorithmic trading strategy, traders should carefully consider factors such as risk management, backtesting, and choice of programming language to optimize the performance of their algorithms.

With the right strategy and tools, traders can achieve success in algorithmic trading and maximize their profits in the financial markets.

Common Strategies Trading System

A common strategies trading system is a set of rules and guidelines that a trader follows to make trading decisions. These strategies are based on technical analysis, fundamental analysis, or a combination of both. The goal of a trading system is to maximize profits and minimize losses by identifying high-probability trading opportunities.

There are many different types of trading systems, each with its own unique set of rules and guidelines. Some common strategies trading systems include trend-following systems, mean-reversion systems, breakout systems, and momentum systems. Each of these systems has its own advantages and disadvantages, and traders must choose the system that best fits their trading style and risk tolerance.

One of the most common strategies trading systems is trend-following. Trend-following systems are based on the idea that markets tend to move in trends, and that by following these trends, traders can profit from the market's momentum. Trend-following systems use technical indicators such as moving averages, trendlines, and price patterns to identify the direction of the trend and enter trades in the direction of the trend.

Another common strategies trading system is mean-reversion. Mean-reversion systems are based on the idea that prices tend to revert to their average value over time. Mean-reversion systems use technical indicators such as

Bollinger Bands, RSI, and MACD to identify overbought and oversold conditions in the market and enter trades when prices are likely to revert to their average value.

Breakout systems are another common strategies trading system. Breakout systems are based on the idea that when prices break out of a trading range, they tend to continue in the direction of the breakout. Breakout systems use technical indicators such as support and resistance levels, trendlines, and price patterns to identify breakout opportunities and enter trades in the direction of the breakout.

Momentum systems are also a common strategies trading system. Momentum systems are based on the idea that prices tend to continue in the direction of their momentum. Momentum systems use technical indicators such as moving averages, MACD, and stochastic oscillators to identify strong trends and enter trades in the direction of the trend.

Regardless of the type of trading system used, there are several common strategies that traders can use to maximize profits and minimize losses. One common strategy is to use proper risk management techniques such as setting stop-loss orders and position sizing to limit losses and protect profits. Another common strategy is to use multiple timeframes to confirm trading signals and increase the probability of success.

In addition to risk management and multiple timeframes, traders can also use technical analysis and fundamental analysis to identify high-probability trading opportunities.

Technical analysis involves analyzing price charts and technical indicators to identify trends and patterns in the market. Fundamental analysis involves analyzing economic data, company earnings reports, and other factors that can impact the value of a security.

By combining technical analysis, fundamental analysis, risk management, and multiple timeframes, traders can create a common strategies trading system that maximizes profits and minimizes losses. It is important for traders to backtest their trading system on historical data to ensure that it is profitable and reliable before using it in live trading.

Overall, a common strategies trading system is a valuable tool for traders to use to make informed trading decisions and maximize profits. By following a set of rules and guidelines based on technical analysis, fundamental analysis, risk management, and multiple timeframes, traders can increase their chances of success in the market.

Chapter 5: Designing a Trading Bot

In this chapter, we will discuss the process of designing a trading bot in the language of your choice. Designing a trading bot involves a combination of technical skills, market knowledge, and strategic thinking. By following the steps outlined in this chapter, you can create a trading bot that is tailored to your specific trading goals and preferences.

The first step in designing a trading bot is to define your trading strategy. This involves determining the types of assets you want to trade, the timeframes you want to trade on, and the indicators you want to use to make trading decisions. Your trading strategy should be based on a combination of technical analysis, fundamental analysis, and market sentiment.

Once you have defined your trading strategy, the next step is to choose a programming language for your trading bot. There are many programming languages that can be used to create trading bots, including Python, Java, C++, and JavaScript. The language you choose will depend on your programming skills, the availability of libraries and APIs for trading, and the specific features you want to include in your bot.

After choosing a programming language, the next step is to design the architecture of your trading bot. This involves breaking down your trading strategy into a series of logical steps that can be implemented in code. You will need to decide how your bot will interact with the market, how it will make trading decisions, and how it will manage risk.

Once you have designed the architecture of your trading bot, the next step is to implement the code. This involves writing the algorithms that will execute your trading strategy, integrating with market data sources and trading platforms, and testing the bot to ensure that it functions as intended. This process can be time-consuming and complex, but it is essential for creating a successful trading bot.

After implementing the code, the final step is to optimize and backtest your trading bot. Optimization involves fine-tuning the parameters of your trading strategy to maximize profitability and minimize risk. Backtesting involves running your bot on historical market data to see how it would have performed in the past. By optimizing and backtesting your trading bot, you can identify any weaknesses in your strategy and make adjustments before deploying it in live trading.

Designing a trading bot in the language of your choice is a challenging but rewarding process. By following the steps outlined in this chapter, you can create a trading bot that is tailored to your specific trading goals and preferences. Remember to define your trading strategy, choose a programming language, design the architecture of your bot, implement the code, and optimize and backtest your bot before deploying it in live trading. With careful planning and execution, you can create a trading bot that can help you achieve your trading goals and improve your overall profitability.

Bot Architecture and Design Principles

In recent years, the use of bots has become increasingly popular in various industries, including customer service, healthcare, and e-commerce. Bots, also known as chatbots or conversational agents, are computer programs that simulate human conversation through artificial intelligence. They are designed to interact with users in a natural language format, providing information, answering questions, and completing tasks.

Bot architecture and design principles play a crucial role in the development and operation of effective bots. In this article, we will discuss the key components of bot architecture and the design principles that should be considered when creating a bot in the language.

Bot Architecture
Bot architecture refers to the structure and components of a bot system. A well-designed bot architecture is essential for the bot to function efficiently and effectively. The following are the key components of bot architecture:

User Interface: The user interface is the front-end component of the bot that allows users to interact with the bot. It includes the chat window or interface where users can type or speak their queries and receive responses from the bot.

Natural Language Understanding (NLU): NLU is the component of the bot that interprets and understands the user's input. It uses natural language processing techniques to analyze the user's text or speech and extract the meaning and intent behind it.

Dialogue Management: Dialogue management is responsible for managing the conversation flow between the bot and the user. It determines the bot's responses based on the user's input and maintains context throughout the conversation.

Knowledge Base: The knowledge base is a repository of information that the bot uses to provide responses to user queries. It can include FAQs, product information, troubleshooting guides, and other relevant content.

Integration: Integration refers to the process of connecting the bot with external systems and services, such as databases, APIs, and third-party applications. It allows the bot to access and retrieve information from these sources to provide accurate and up-to-date responses to users.

Design Principles
When designing a bot in the language, several principles should be considered to ensure that the bot is user-friendly, efficient, and effective. The following are some key design principles for bot architecture:

Understand User Intent: To design a successful bot, it is essential to understand the user's intent and provide relevant and accurate responses. This can be achieved through effective NLU and dialogue management techniques that analyze the user's input and determine the context and meaning behind it.

Provide Clear and Concise Responses: Bots should provide clear and concise responses to user queries to ensure that users understand the information provided. Avoid using complex language or jargon and aim to communicate in a conversational and engaging manner.

Maintain Context: Dialogue management plays a crucial role in maintaining context throughout the conversation. The bot should remember previous interactions with the user and use this information to provide personalized responses and recommendations.

Offer Multiple Interaction Channels: Bots should be designed to interact with users through multiple channels, such as text, voice, and multimedia. This allows users to choose their preferred mode of communication and enhances the overall user experience.

Provide Feedback and Error Handling: Bots should provide feedback to users to acknowledge their input and guide them through the conversation. Error handling mechanisms should be in place to handle misunderstandings, incorrect inputs, and other issues that may arise during the interaction.

Personalize the User Experience: Personalization is key to creating a positive user experience with the bot. Use data analytics and machine learning techniques to personalize responses based on the user's preferences, behavior, and past interactions.

Ensure Security and Privacy: Security and privacy are

paramount when designing a bot system. Implement robust security measures to protect user data and ensure compliance with data protection regulations, such as GDPR.

Bot architecture and design principles are essential for creating successful and effective bots in the language. By following these principles and considering the key components of bot architecture, developers can design bots that provide valuable and engaging experiences for users. As the use of bots continues to grow, it is important toprioritize user-centric design and incorporate the latest technologies and best practices to create innovative and user-friendly bot systems.

Implementing Functions trading bot with python - scripts

In the world of cryptocurrency trading, automation has become increasingly popular as traders seek to take advantage of the fast-paced nature of the market. One way to automate trading is through the use of trading bots, which are programs that execute trades on behalf of the user based on predefined criteria.

Python is a popular programming language for building trading bots due to its simplicity and flexibility. In this article, we will discuss how to implement functions in a trading bot using Python, with a focus on script examples.

Functions are a key concept in Python that allow you to encapsulate a block of code that can be reused multiple times. In the context of a trading bot, functions can be used to define specific trading strategies or actions that the bot should take based on certain conditions.

To illustrate how functions can be implemented in a trading bot, let's consider a simple example where we want to create a function that buys a certain cryptocurrency when its price crosses a certain threshold.

First, we need to import the necessary libraries for interacting with the cryptocurrency exchange API and handling data. We can use the popular requests library for making HTTP requests and the pandas library for working with data.

```python
import requests
import pandas as pd
```

Next, we define our function for buying the cryptocurrency when the price crosses a certain threshold. We will call this function `buy_crypto`.

```python
def buy_crypto(symbol, threshold):
# Get the current price of the cryptocurrency
url = f'https://api.exchange.com/price/{symbol}'
response = requests.get(url)
data = response.json()
current_price = data['price']

# Check if the current price is above the threshold
if current_price > threshold:
# Place a buy order for the cryptocurrency
# (code for placing buy order goes here)
print(f'Buying {symbol} at {current_price}')
else:
print(f'Price of {symbol} is below threshold')
```

In this function, we first retrieve the current price of the cryptocurrency using the exchange API. We then compare this price to the threshold value provided as an argument to the function. If the current price is above the threshold, we print a message indicating that we are buying the cryptocurrency. Otherwise, we print a message indicating that the price is below the threshold.

Now that we have defined our `buy_crypto` function, we can call it with the symbol of the cryptocurrency we want to trade and the threshold price.

```python
buy_crypto('BTC', 50000)
```

This will execute the function and print a message indicating whether the cryptocurrency was bought or not based on the current price and the threshold value.

Functions can be further extended to include additional logic and conditions based on the requirements of the trading strategy. For example, you could add a stop-loss condition to sell the cryptocurrency if the price drops below a certain level.

In addition to defining functions for specific trading actions, you can also create functions to retrieve historical data, analyze market trends, and generate trading signals. These functions can then be combined to form a complete trading strategy within the bot.

Overall, implementing functions in a trading bot using Python allows for modular and reusable code that can be easily maintained and extended. By breaking down the trading logic into smaller functions, you can create a more flexible and scalable bot that can adapt to changing market conditions.

Functions play a crucial role in the development of a trading bot in Python. By encapsulating specific trading actions and conditions within functions, you can create a more organized and efficient bot that iseasier to manage and update. With the right combination of functions and strategies, you can build a powerful trading bot that can help you navigate the complex world of cryptocurrency trading.

Chapter 6 : Backtesting Strategies automation with python

Backtesting is a crucial step in the development and evaluation of trading strategies. It involves testing a strategy on historical data to see how it would have performed in the past. This allows traders to assess the viability of their strategies and make any necessary adjustments before risking real money in the markets.

Automation of backtesting strategies can greatly streamline the process and make it more efficient. By using Python, a popular programming language in the financial industry, traders can automate the backtesting of theirstrategies and save time and effort.

There are several advantages to automating backtesting strategies with Python. Firstly, it allows traders to test multiple strategies simultaneously, saving time and increasing productivity. Python's versatility and flexibility make it easy to implement complex trading strategies and analyze large amounts of data quickly.

Secondly, automation reduces the risk of human error. By removing the manual element from the backtesting process, traders can eliminate mistakes and ensure that their results are accurate and reliable. This is especially important when testing complex strategies that involve multiple parameters and variables.

Another benefit of automating backtesting strategies with

Python is the ability to backtest strategies in real-time. This allows traders to test their strategies on current market data and make adjustments as needed. By automating the process, traders can stay ahead of the curve and adapt to changing market conditions more effectively.

To automate backtesting strategies with Python, traders can use a variety of libraries and tools that are available. One popular library is Pandas, which is a powerful data manipulation tool that allows traders to easily import and analyze historical data. Another useful library is NumPy, which provides support for numerical calculations and array manipulation.

In addition, traders can use backtesting frameworks such as Backtrader and Zipline, which provide a set of tools and functions specifically designed for backtesting trading strategies. These frameworks make it easy to implement and test strategies in Python and provide a standardized approach to backtesting.

When automating backtesting strategies with Python, traders should follow a systematic approach to ensure that their strategies are tested thoroughly and accurately. This involves defining clear objectives and criteria for the backtest, selecting appropriate data and time periods, and setting up the necessary parameters and variables for the strategy.

Traders should also consider the performance metrics that they will use to evaluate the strategy, such as profit and loss, Sharpe ratio, and maximum drawdown. By measuring these metrics, traders can assess the effectiveness of their strategies and make informed decisions about their trading approach.

Automating backtesting strategies with Python is a valuable tool for traders looking to develop and evaluate their trading strategies. By using Python's powerful capabilities and a systematic approach to backtesting, traders can improve their trading performance and make more informed decisions in the markets.

Importance of Backtesting Trading System

Backtesting is a crucial component of any successful trading strategy. It involves testing a trading system using historical data to see how it would have performed in the past. By analyzing past performance, traders can gain valuable insights into the effectiveness of their strategy and make informed decisions about its future use.

There are several reasons why backtesting is important for traders. First and foremost, it helps traders evaluate the profitability of their trading system. By testing a strategy over a period of time, traders can determine whether it would have generated profits or losses in the past. This information is essential for assessing the viability of a trading system and making adjustments as needed.

In addition to profitability, backtesting can also help traders identify potential weaknesses in their strategy. By analyzing past performance, traders can pinpoint areas where their strategy may have underperformed and make improvements to enhance its effectiveness. This process of continuous improvement is essential for staying ahead in the fast-paced world of trading.

Furthermore, backtesting can help traders gain confidence in their strategy. By seeing how a trading system would have performed in the past, traders can develop a sense of trust in their strategy and its ability to generate profits. This confidence can be invaluable when making decisions in the heat of the moment, as traders can rely on the data from their backtesting to guide their actions.

Another important benefit of backtesting is risk management. By testing a trading system using historical data,traders can assess the potential risks associated with their strategy and take steps to mitigate them. This can help traders avoid large losses and protect their capital, ensuring long-term success in the market.

Moreover, backtesting can help traders optimize their strategy for maximum efficiency. By analyzing past performance, traders can identify the most profitable trades and make adjustments to their strategy to capitalize on these opportunities. This process of optimization can lead to higher returns and greater success in the market.

Overall, backtesting is an essential tool for traders looking to develop and maintain a successful trading strategy. By testing a strategy using historical data, traders can evaluate its profitability, identify weaknesses, gain confidence, manage risk, and optimize for maximum efficiency. These benefits can help traders achieve long-term success in the market and stay ahead of the competition.

Tools and Libraries for Backtesting Trading system

Backtesting is a crucial step in the development and evaluation of a trading system. It involves testing the performance of a trading strategy using historical data to see how it would have performed in the past. This helps traders to assess the viability of their strategies and make necessary adjustments before risking real money in live trading.

To conduct backtesting effectively, traders need access to tools and libraries that can help them analyze historical data, simulate trades, and evaluate performance metrics. There are several tools and libraries available in the market that cater to the needs of traders looking to backtest their trading systems. In this article, we will explore some of the popular tools and libraries used for backtesting trading systems in different programming languages.

Python:
Python is a popular programming language among traders and quantitative analysts due to its simplicity and versatility. There are several libraries available in Python that can be used for backtesting trading systems. Some of the popular ones include:

Backtrader: Backtrader is a flexible and easy-to-use Python library for backtesting trading strategies. It allows traders to create and test complex trading strategies using historical data. Backtrader supports multiple data sources, including CSV files, Pandas DataFrames, and live data feeds, making it a versatile tool for backtesting.

PyAlgoTrade: PyAlgoTrade is another Python library that is widely used for backtesting trading systems. It provides a simple and intuitive interface for creating and testing trading strategies. PyAlgoTrade supports multiple data sources and allows traders to customize their backtesting process by defining their own data feeds and indicators.

Zipline: Zipline is an open-source backtesting library developed by Quantopian, a popular platform for algorithmic trading. Zipline is built on top of Pandas and NumPy, making it a powerful tool for backtesting trading strategies. It supports event-driven backtesting and allows traders to test their strategies on historical data.

R:
R is another popular programming language among traders and data scientists for backtesting trading systems. There are several libraries available in R that can be used for backtesting, including:

quantstrat: quantstrat is a powerful backtesting framework for R that allows traders to create and test trading strategies using historical data. It supports event-driven backtesting and provides a wide range of performance metrics to evaluate the performance of trading strategies. quantstrat is highly customizable and allows traders to define their own trading rules and indicators.

PerformanceAnalytics: PerformanceAnalytics is a popular R package that provides a wide range of tools for analyzing the performance of trading strategies. It allows traders to calculate various performance metrics, such as Sharpe ratio, maximum drawdown, and annualized return. PerformanceAnalytics is a valuable tool for evaluating the risk and return of trading strategies.

MATLAB:
MATLAB is a widely used programming language in the finance industry for backtesting trading systems. There are several toolboxes available in MATLAB that can be used for backtesting, including:

Financial Toolbox: The Financial Toolbox in MATLAB provides a wide range of functions for analyzing financial data and backtesting trading strategies. It supports event-driven backtesting and allows traders to test their strategies on historical data. The Financial Toolbox is a valuable tool for creating and testing complex trading strategies.

Econometrics Toolbox: The Econometrics Toolbox in MATLAB provides a wide range of functions for analyzing time series data and estimating econometric models. It allows traders to model the behavior of financial markets and test the performance of trading strategies using historical data. The Econometrics Toolbox is a valuable tool for backtesting trading systems.

Java:
Java is a popular programming language for developing trading systems due to its speed and scalability. There are several libraries available in Java that can be used for backtesting, including:

JForex API: JForex API is a Java library developed by Dukascopy, a popular forex broker. It allows traders to create and test trading strategies using historical data from the Dukascopy trading platform. JForex API supports event-driven backtesting and provides a wide range of performance metrics to evaluate the performance of trading strategies.

QuantLib: QuantLib is an open-source library for quantitative finance developed in C++ but also available in Java. It provides a wide range of functions for modeling financial instruments and analyzing historical data. QuantLib is a powerful tool for backtesting trading systems and allows traders to test their strategies on historical data.

Backtesting trading systems is an essential step in the development and evaluation of trading strategies. Traders need access to tools and libraries that can help them analyze historical data, simulate trades, and evaluate performance metrics. There are several tools and libraries available in different programming languages that cater to the needs of traders looking to backtest their trading systems. Whether you prefer Python, R, MATLAB, or Java, there is a wide range of options available to help you backtest your trading strategies effectively. Choose the tool or library that best suits your needs

Chapter 7: Data Collection and Analysis in Trading

Data collection and analysis are crucial components of successful trading in the financial markets. In this chapter, we will explore the importance of gathering and analyzing data to make informed trading decisions.

Data Collection:

Data collection is the process of gathering information from various sources to use in trading analysis. There are several types of data that traders may collect, including market data, economic data, and company-specific data.

Market data includes information on price movements, volume, and other relevant statistics for various financial instruments. This data is typically obtained from exchanges, financial news sources, and trading platforms.

Economic data refers to reports on the health of the economy, such as GDP growth, unemployment rates, and inflation. This data can have a significant impact on the financial markets and should be closely monitored by traders.

Company-specific data includes information on individual companies, such as earnings reports, product launches, and management changes. This data can help traders assess the health and potential of a particular company's stock.

In addition to these types of data, traders may also collect data on technical indicators, sentiment indicators, and other factors that can influence market movements.

Data Analysis:

Once data has been collected, traders must analyze it to identify trends, patterns, and potential trading opportunities. There are several methods of data analysis that traders may use, including fundamental analysis, technical analysis, and quantitative analysis.

Fundamental analysis involves examining economic and company-specific data to assess the intrinsic value of a financial instrument. This analysis can help traders determine whether a stock is undervalued or overvalued and make informed investment decisions.

Technical analysis, on the other hand, involves studying price charts and technical indicators to identify trends and patterns in market movements. This analysis can help traders predict future price movements and time their trades accordingly.

Quantitative analysis involves using mathematical models and statistical techniques to analyze data and develop trading strategies. This analysis can help traders identify correlations and relationships between different factors and optimize their trading performance.

In addition to these methods, traders may also use sentiment analysis, which involves analyzing market sentiment and investor behavior to gauge market sentiment and predict future price movements.

Data Management:

Effective data management is essential for successful trading. Traders must organize and store data in a way that is easily accessible and secure. This may involve using data management software, cloud storage solutions, and other tools to ensure that data is accurate and up-to-date.

Traders should also be aware of data privacy and security concerns when collecting and storing data. It is important to only collect data from reputable sources and take steps to protect sensitive information from unauthorized access.

Furthermore, traders should regularly review and update their data collection and analysis processes to ensure that they are using the most relevant and accurate information to make trading decisions.

Data collection and analysis are essential components of successful trading in the financial markets. By gathering and analyzing data from various sources, traders can make informed decisions and improve their trading performance. Effective data management is also crucial to ensure that data is accurate, secure, and easily accessible. By using a combination of fundamental, technical, and quantitative analysis, traders can develop effective trading strategies and maximize their profits in the markets.

APIs for Stock and Crypto Data for Trading System

In today's fast-paced and ever-changing financial markets, having access to real-time and accurate data is crucial for making informed trading decisions. This is where APIs for stock and crypto data come into play. These APIs provide developers with the ability to access and integrate market data into their trading systems, allowing them to stay ahead of the competition and make more profitable trades.

Stock APIs provide developers with access to a wealth of information about publicly traded companies, including stock prices, trading volumes, historical data, and more. By using stock APIs, traders can quickly and easily retrieve the latest market data for any given stock, allowing them to make informed decisions about when to buy or sell.

Crypto APIs, on the other hand, provide developers with access to data about cryptocurrencies, including prices, trading volumes, market capitalization, and more. With the rise of cryptocurrencies in recent years, having access to real-time data about these digital assets is essential for traders looking to capitalize on this emerging market.

By integrating stock and crypto APIs into their trading systems, developers can create powerful tools that give them a competitive edge in the market. Whether they are building automated trading algorithms, conducting technical analysis, or simply keeping track of their portfolios, APIs for stock and crypto data provide the necessary information to make informed decisions and maximize profits.

One of the key benefits of using APIs for stock and crypto data is the ability to access real-time information.With traditional methods of data collection, traders often have to rely on delayed data feeds or manual data entry, which can lead to missed opportunities and inaccurate information. APIs, on the other hand, provide instant access to the latest market data, allowing traders to make decisions based on up-to-date information.

Another benefit of using APIs for stock and crypto data is the ability to automate trading strategies. By integrating APIs into their trading systems, developers can create algorithms that automatically execute trades based on predefined criteria. This not only saves time and reduces the risk of human error but also allows traders to take advantage of opportunities that may arise when they are not actively monitoring the market.

In addition to real-time data and automation capabilities, APIs for stock and crypto data also offer a wide range of market indicators and analytics tools. These tools allow traders to conduct technical analysis, track market trends, and identify potential trading opportunities. By using APIs to access this information, traders can make more informed decisions and increase their chances of success in the market.

Overall, APIs for stock and crypto data play a crucial role in modern trading systems. By providing access to real-time information, automation capabilities, and advanced analytics tools, these APIs empower traders to make smarter decisions and stay ahead of the competition. Whether you are a seasoned trader looking to enhance your strategies or a developer building a new trading system, integrating APIs for stock and crypto data is essential for success in today's financial markets.

Handling Large Datasets in trading

Handling large datasets in trading is a crucial aspect of the financial industry. With the increasing amount of data available, traders need to be able to effectively manage and analyze large datasets in order to make informed decisions and stay ahead of the competition. In this article, we will explore the challenges of handling large datasets in trading and provide some tips on how to effectively manage and analyze this data.

One of the biggest challenges of handling large datasets in trading is the sheer volume of data that needs to be processed. With the advent of high-frequency trading and algorithmic trading, traders now have access to a massive amount of data that needs to be analyzed in real-time. This can be overwhelming for traders, especially those who are not equipped with the right tools and techniques to handle such large datasets.

Another challenge of handling large datasets in trading is the complexity of the data itself. Financial data is often messy and unstructured, making it difficult to extract meaningful insights from it. Traders need to be able to clean and preprocess the data before they can analyze it, which can be a time-consuming and tedious process.

In addition to the volume and complexity of the data, traders also need to consider the speed at which the data is being generated. In the fast-paced world of trading, decisions need to be made quickly in order to capitalize on market opportunities. This means that traders need to be able to analyze large datasets in real-time and make split-second decisions based on the insights they derive from the data.

So how can traders effectively handle large datasets in trading? One approach is to use advanced data analytics tools and techniques to streamline the process of data analysis. These tools can help traders clean and preprocess the data, perform complex analyses, and generate actionable insights in a fraction of the time it would take to do manually.

Another approach is to leverage cloud computing and big data technologies to scale up the processing power needed to handle large datasets. By using cloud-based services and distributed computing platforms, traders can quickly analyze massive amounts of data and extract insights in real-time.

Traders can also use machine learning and artificial intelligence algorithms to automate the process of data analysis. These algorithms can quickly identify patterns and trends in the data, allowing traders to make more informed decisions based on the insights they generate.

In addition to using advanced tools and technologies, traders also need to have a solid understanding of the underlying data and the factors that can influence market movements. By staying informed about market trends, economic indicators, and other relevant factors, traders can make more accurate predictions and better manage their portfolios.

Ultimately, handling large datasets in trading requires a combination of advanced tools, technologies, and market knowledge. By leveraging these resources effectively, traders can gain a competitive edge in the financial markets and make more informed decisions that lead to greater profits.

Handling large datasets in trading is a challenging but essential task for traders in the financial industry. By using advanced tools and technologies, staying informed about market trends, and leveraging their market knowledge, traders can effectively manage and analyze large datasets to make more informed decisions and stay ahead of the competition.

Chapter 8: Data Preprocessing and Cleaning in Trading

In the world of trading, having clean and accurate data is essential for making informed decisions and maximizing profits. Data preprocessing and cleaning are crucial steps in the data analysis process, as they helpensure that the data used for trading is accurate, complete, and reliable.

Data preprocessing involves transforming raw data into a format that is suitable for analysis. This process includes tasks such as removing duplicates, handling missing values, and normalizing data. By cleaning and preprocessing data, traders can reduce errors andbiases in their analysis, leading to more accurate predictions and trading strategies.

One of the first steps in data preprocessing is identifying and removing duplicates. Duplicates can skew analysis results and lead to inaccurate conclusions. By removing duplicates, traders can ensure that each data point is unique and representative of the underlying market conditions.

Handling missing values is another important aspect of data preprocessing. Missing values can occur for a variety of reasons, such as data collection errors or system failures. Traders must decide how to handle missing values, whether by imputing them with a suitable value or removing them altogether. Imputing missing values can help preserve the integrity of the dataset and ensure that no relevant information is lost.

Normalization is another key step in data preprocessing. Normalizing data involves scaling numerical features to a standard range, such as between 0 and 1. This process helps ensure that all features are on a similar scale, making it easier to compare and analyze them. Normalization can also help improve the performance of machine learning models by reducing the impact of outliers and improving convergence.

In addition to data preprocessing, data cleaning is also an essential part of the trading process. Data cleaning involves identifying and correcting errors in the dataset, such as incorrect values or outliers. By cleaning the data, traders can ensure that the data used for analysis is accurate and reliable.

One common technique for data cleaning is outlier detection. Outliers are data points that deviate significantly from the rest of the dataset and can skew analysis results. By identifying and removing outliers, traders can ensure that their analysis is based on accurate and representative data.

Another important aspect of data cleaning is data validation. Data validation involves checking the integrity and accuracy of the data, such as verifying that numerical values are within a certain range or that categorical values are correctly labeled. By validating the data, traders can identify and correct errors before they impact the analysis.

In the world of trading, data preprocessing and cleaning

are essential steps in the data analysis process. By ensuring that the data used for trading is accurate, complete, and reliable, traders can make informed decisions and maximize profits. By removing duplicates, handling missing values, normalizing data, and cleaning errors, traders can improve the quality of their analysis and develop more effective trading strategies.

Techniques for Data Cleaning with python for trading

Data cleaning is an essential process in any trading strategy, as the quality of the data used directly impacts the accuracy and effectiveness of the trading model. In this article, we will explore various techniques for data cleaning with Python specifically tailored for trading purposes.

Data Importing:
The first step in data cleaning is importing the raw data into Python. This can be done using libraries such as pandas, which provides powerful tools for data manipulation and analysis. The data can be imported from various sources such as CSV files, databases, or web APIs.

Data Exploration:
Once the data is imported, the next step is to explore the data to understand its structure and identify any anomalies or missing values. This can be done by using descriptive statistics, visualizations, and data profiling techniques. It is important to have a good understanding of the data before proceeding with the cleaning process.

Handling Missing Values:
Missing values are a common issue in trading data and can significantly impact the performance of the trading model. There are several techniques for handling missing values, such as imputation, deletion, or interpolation. The choice of technique depends on the nature of the data and the

trading strategy being used.

Outlier Detection:
Outliers are data points that deviate significantly from the rest of the data and can distort the analysis. Detecting and handling outliers is crucial for building an accurate trading model. There are various techniques for outlier detection, such as Z-score, IQR, and clustering-based methods.

Data Transformation:
Data transformation involves converting the raw data into a format that is suitable for analysis and modeling. This can include scaling, normalization, encoding categorical variables, and feature engineering. Data transformation is essential for improving the performance of the trading model.

Data Aggregation:
Data aggregation involves combining multiple data points into a single value, such as calculating averages, sums, or other statistics. Aggregating the data can help reduce noise and improve the signal-to-noise ratio in the trading model. Aggregation techniques can be used to create new features that capture important patterns in the data.

Data Filtering:
Data filtering involves removing irrelevant or redundant data points from the dataset. This can help reduce the complexity of the data and improve the efficiency of the trading model. Filtering techniques can be used to focus on relevant data points that are most likely to impact the trading strategy.

Data Normalization:
Data normalization is the process of scaling the data to a standard range, such as between 0 and 1. Normalizing the data can help improve the performance of machine learning algorithms and reduce the impact of outliers. There are various normalization techniques, such as Min-Max scaling, Z-score normalization, and robust scaling.

Data Resampling:

Data resampling involves changing the frequency or time period of the data points. This can be useful for aligning the data with the trading strategy or for handling irregularly spaced data. Resampling techniques include upsampling, downsampling, and interpolation.

Data Validation:
Data validation is the process of ensuring that the data meets certain quality standards and is suitable for analysis. This can involve checking for consistency, accuracy, and completeness of the data. Data validation is essential for building a reliable trading model that can generate consistent results.

Data cleaning is a critical step in the trading process that can significantly impact the performance of the trading model. By using the techniques outlined in this article, traders can ensure that their data is clean, accurate, and suitable for analysis.

Python provides powerful tools for data cleaning and manipulation, making it an ideal choice for traders looking to improve their trading strategies. By following best practices for data cleaning, traders can build more reliable and effective trading models that can generate consistent profits.

Ensuring Data Qualityin Trading System with python

Data quality is a critical aspect of any trading system, as accurate and reliable data is essential for making informed decisions and executing successful trades. In this article, we will discuss the importance of ensuring data quality in a trading system and how Python can be used to achieve this goal.

Data quality refers to the accuracy, completeness, consistency, and reliability of data. In the context of a trading system, data quality is particularly important because even small errors or inconsistencies in data can lead to significant losses. For example, if the price data used for making trading decisions is inaccurate, it can result in buying or selling assets at the wrong prices, leading to financial losses.

There are several factors that can affect data quality in a trading system. These include data collection methods, data storage and processing techniques, data cleaning and normalization processes, and data integration with other systems. Ensuring data quality requires a systematic approach that involves identifying potential sources of errors, implementing data validation and verification processes, and continuously monitoring and improving dataquality.

Python is a popular programming language that is widely used in the financial industry for building trading systems and analyzing market data. Python's flexibility, ease of use, and extensive libraries make it an ideal tool for ensuring data quality in a trading system. In this article, we will discuss some best practices for ensuring data quality in a trading system using Python.

Data Collection and Storage
The first step in ensuring data quality in a trading system is to collect and store data from reliable sources. It is important to use reputable data providers and APIs to ensure the accuracy and reliability of the data. Python provides several libraries for accessing and retrieving data from various sources, such as pandas, requests, and BeautifulSoup.

Once the data is collected, it should be stored in a secure and organized manner. Python's pandas library can be used for storing and manipulating data in tabular format, making it easy to access and analyze the data. It is important to regularly update and maintain the data to ensure its accuracy and completeness.

Data Cleaning and Normalization
Data cleaning and normalization are essential steps in ensuring data quality in a trading system. Data cleaning involves identifying and correcting errors, inconsistencies, and missing values in the data. Python provides several libraries, such as pandas and NumPy, for cleaning and preprocessing data.

Normalization is the process of standardizing data values to a common scale or format. This helps to eliminate biases and inconsistencies in the data, making it easier to compare and analyze. Python's scikit-learn library provides tools for normalizing data and preparing it for analysis.

Data Validation and Verification
Data validation and verification are important processes for ensuring the accuracy and reliability of the data in a trading system. Data validation involves checking the integrity and consistency of the data, while data verification involves comparing the data with external sources to ensure its accuracy.

Python provides several libraries and tools for data validation and verification, such as pandas, NumPy, and scikit-learn. These libraries can be used to perform statistical analysis, data profiling, and anomaly detection toidentify and correct errors in the data.

Data Integration and Analysis
Once the data is collected, cleaned, and validated, it can be integrated into the trading system for analysis and decision-making. Python provides several libraries for data analysis and visualization, such as pandas, NumPy, and Matplotlib, which can be used to analyze market trends, identify trading opportunities, and optimize tradingstrategies.

Data integration involves combining data from multiple sources to create a unified view of the market. Python's pandas library provides tools for merging, joining, and aggregating data from different sources, making it easy to integrate data for analysis.

Continuous Monitoring and Improvement

Ensuring data quality is an ongoing process that requires continuous monitoring and improvement. It is important to regularly review and audit the data to identify and correct errors, inconsistencies, and biases. Python provides tools for automated data quality monitoring and alerting, such as pandas profiling and data quality libraries.

It is also important to involve domain experts and stakeholders in the data quality process to ensure that the data meets the requirements and expectations of the trading system. Regular communication and collaboration with data providers, analysts, and traders can help to identify and address data quality issues in a timely manner.

Ensuring data quality in a trading system is essential for making informed decisions and executing successful trades. Python provides a powerful set of tools and libraries for collecting, cleaning, validating, and analyzing data, making it an ideal choice for ensuring data quality in a trading system.

By following best practices and implementing systematic processes, traders can improve the accuracy and reliability of their data, leading to more profitable trading strategies and better investment decisions.

Chapter 9: Technical Analysis with Python in trading

Technical analysis is a popular method used by traders to forecast future price movements based on historicaldata. In this chapter, we will explore how to perform technical analysis using Python in trading. Python is a powerful programming language that is widely used in the financial industry for data analysis and algorithmictrading.

One of the key components of technical analysis is the use of charts to visualize historical price data. Python has several libraries that make it easy to plot charts, such as Matplotlib and Seaborn. These libraries allow traders to create various types of charts, including line charts, bar charts, and candlestick charts, which are commonly usedin technical analysis.

Another important aspect of technical analysis is the use of technical indicators to identify trends and patterns inprice data. Python has a library called TA-Lib that provides a wide range of technical indicators, such as moving averages, Relative Strength Index (RSI), and Bollinger Bands. These indicators can help traders make informed decisions about when to buy or sell a security.

In addition to plotting charts and using technical indicators, Python can also be used to backtest trading strategies. Backtesting is the process of testing a trading strategy using historical data to see how it would have performed in the past. Python has libraries such as

Backtrader and PyAlgoTrade that make it easy to backtest trading strategies and analyze their performance.

To demonstrate how to perform technical analysis with Python in trading, let's consider a simple example using historical stock price data. We will start by importing the necessary libraries and loading the historical data into a pandas DataFrame.

```python
import pandas as pd
import matplotlib.pyplot as plt import talib

# Load historical stock price data data = pd.read_csv('AAPL.csv')
data['Date'] = pd.to_datetime(data['Date'])
data.set_index('Date', inplace=True)

# Plot the closing price plt.figure(figsize=(10, 6))
plt.plot(data['Close'], label='Close') plt.title('AAPL Closing Price') plt.xlabel('Date')
plt.ylabel('Price') plt.legend() plt.show()
```

Next, we can calculate some technical indicators, such as the 50-day and 200-day moving averages, and plot them on the chart.

```python
# Calculate moving averages
data['MA50'] = talib.SMA(data['Close'], timeperiod=50)
data['MA200'] = talib.SMA(data['Close'], timeperiod=200)

# Plot moving averages plt.figure(figsize=(10, 6))
plt.plot(data['Close'], label='Close') plt.plot(data['MA50'],
label='MA50') plt.plot(data['MA200'], label='MA200')
plt.title('AAPL Moving Averages') plt.xlabel('Date')
plt.ylabel('Price')plt.legend() plt.show()
```

Finally, we can backtest a simple trading strategy based on the moving averages. For example, we can buy when the 50-day moving average crosses above the 200-day moving average and sell when the 50-day moving average crosses below the 200-day moving average.

```python
# Create trading signalsdata['Signal'] = 0
data['Signal'][50:] = np.where(data['MA50'][50:] >
data['MA200'][50:], 1, 0) data['Position'] =
data['Signal'].diff()

# Plot trading signals plt.figure(figsize=(10, 6))
plt.plot(data['Close'], label='Close')
plt.plot(data[data['Position'] == 1].index,
data['MA50'][data['Position'] == 1], '^', markersize=10,
```

```
color='g',lw=0, label='Buy Signal')
plt.plot(data[data['Position']        ==        -1].index,
data['MA50'][data['Position'] == -1], 'v', markersize=10,
color='r',lw=0, label='Sell Signal')
plt.title('AAPL     Trading     Signals')     plt.xlabel('Date')
plt.ylabel('Price')
plt.legend() plt.show()
```

In this example, we have demonstrated how to perform technical analysis with Python in trading using historical stock price data. By plotting charts, calculating technical indicators, and backtesting trading strategies, traders can gain valuable insights into market trends and make more informed decisions about when to buy or sell securities.

Overall, Python is a powerful tool for performing technical analysis in trading due to its ease of use, flexibility, and extensive libraries for data analysis and visualization. By leveraging Python in their trading strategies, traders can improve their decision-making process and potentially increase their profitability in the financial markets.

Key Indicators and Metrics in trading

When it comes to trading, there are a variety of key indicators and metrics that traders use to analyze the market and make informed decisions. These indicators and metrics can help traders identify trends, predict future price movements, and manage risk. In this article, we will discuss some of the most important key indicators and metrics in trading.

One of the most commonly used indicators in trading is moving averages. Moving averages are used to smooth out price data and identify trends. There are two main types of moving averages: simple moving averages (SMA) and exponential moving averages (EMA). SMAs give equal weight to all data points, while EMAs give more weight to recent data points. Traders often use moving averages to identify support and resistance levels, as well as to generate buy and sell signals.

Another important indicator in trading is the Relative Strength Index (RSI). The RSI is a momentum oscillator that measures the speed and change of price movements. The RSI ranges from 0 to 100 and is typically used to identify overbought and oversold conditions in the market. A reading above 70 is considered overbought, while a reading below 30 is considered oversold. Traders often use the RSI to confirm trends and generate buy and sell signals.

The Moving Average Convergence Divergence (MACD) is another popular indicator in trading. The MACD is a trend-following momentum indicator that shows the relationship between two moving averages of a security's price. The MACD is calculated by subtracting the 26-day EMA from the 12-day EMA. Traders often use the MACD to identify trend reversals and generate buy and sell signals.

Volume is also an important metric in trading. Volume measures the number of shares or contracts traded in a security or market during a given period of time. High volume can indicate strong market participation and confirm the validity of a price movement. Low volume, on the other hand, can indicate weak market participation and signal a lack of conviction in a price movement. Traders often use volume to confirm trendsand identify potential reversals.

Volatility is another key metric in trading. Volatility measures the degree of variation in a security's price over time. High volatility can indicate greater potential for profit, but also greater risk. Low volatility, on the other hand, can indicate lower risk, but also lower potential for profit. Traders often use volatility to determine position size and set stop-loss orders.

Risk management is another important aspect of trading that involves key indicators and metrics. Traders often use metrics such as the Sharpe ratio and the Sortino ratio to measure the risk-adjusted return of a trading strategy. The Sharpe ratio measures the excess return of a strategy relative to its risk, while the Sortino ratio measures the excess return of a strategy relative to its downside risk. Traders often use these ratios to evaluatethe performance of a trading strategy and compare it to other strategies.

There are a variety of key indicators and metrics that traders use in trading to analyze the market, identify trends, predict future price movements, and manage risk. Moving averages, the RSI, the MACD, volume, volatility, and risk management metrics such as the Sharpe ratio and the Sortino ratio are just a few examples of the many indicators and metrics that traders use in trading. By understanding and using these key indicators and metrics effectively, traders can make informed decisions and improve their trading performance.

Implementing Technical Indicators in Trading with Python - scripts

Technical indicators are powerful tools used by traders to analyze market trends and make informed decisions about when to buy or sell assets. These indicators are mathematical calculations based on historical price and volume data, which can help traders identify potential entry and exit points for their trades. In this article, we will explore how to implement technical indicators in trading using Python, along with some example scripts to demonstrate their usage.

Python is a popular programming language among traders and developers due to its simplicity, flexibility, and extensive libraries for data analysis and visualization. By leveraging Python's capabilities, traders can easily implement and test various technical indicators to improve their trading strategies and make more informed decisions.

There are several technical indicators commonly used by traders, such as moving averages, relative strength index (RSI), stochastic oscillator, MACD (Moving Average Convergence Divergence), and Bollinger Bands, among others. These indicators can provide valuable insights into market trends, momentum, and volatility, helping traders to identify potential opportunities and manage risk effectively.

To implement technical indicators in trading with Python, we first need to gather historical price and volume data for the asset we want to analyze. This data can be obtained from various sources, such as financial websites, APIs, or directly from a brokerage platform. Once we have the data, we can calculate the desired technical indicators using Python libraries such as NumPy, pandas, and matplotlib for data manipulation, analysis, and visualization.

Let's walk through an example of implementing a simple moving average crossover strategy using Python. The moving average crossover strategy involves using two moving averages with different periods (e.g., 50-day and 200-day moving averages) to generate buy and sell signals based on their crossover points.

```python
import pandas as pd import numpy as np
import matplotlib.pyplot as plt

# Load historical price data
data = pd.read_csv('historical_data.csv') data['Date'] = pd.to_datetime(data['Date'])       data.set_index('Date', inplace=True)

# Calculate moving averages
data['MA50'] = data['Close'].rolling(window=50).mean()
data['MA200']                                        = data['Close'].rolling(window=200).mean()

# Generate buy/sell signals
data['Signal'] = np.where(data['MA50'] > data['MA200'], 1, 0)data['Position'] = data['Signal'].diff()
```

Plotting the moving averages and buy/sell signals

```
plt.figure(figsize=(12,        6))        plt.plot(data['Close'],
label='Close  Price')  plt.plot(data['MA50'],  label='50-day
MA') plt.plot(data['MA200'], label='200-day MA')
plt.plot(data[data['Position']        ==        1].index,
data['MA50'][data['Position']  ==  1],  '^',  markersize=10,
color='g',lw=0, label='Buy Signal')
plt.plot(data[data['Position']        ==        -1].index,
data['MA50'][data['Position']  ==  -1],  'v',  markersize=10,
color='r',lw=0, label='Sell Signal')
plt.title('Moving  Average  Crossover  Strategy')  plt.legend()
plt.show()
```

In this script, we first load historical price data from a CSV file and calculate the 50-day and 200-day moving averages for the asset's closing prices. We then generate buy and sell signals based on the crossover points of the moving averages and plot them along with the closing prices to visualize the trading strategy.

This is just a simple example of implementing a technical indicator in trading with Python. Traders can explore and experiment with various technical indicators and strategies to find what works best for their trading style and risk tolerance. It is essential to backtest these strategies using historical data to evaluate their performance and make necessary adjustments before applying them in live trading.

In addition to moving averages, traders can also implement other technical indicators like RSI, stochastic

106

oscillator, MACD, and Bollinger Bands using Python. These indicators can provide additional insights into market trends, momentum, and volatility, helping traders to make more informed decisions and improve their trading performance.

```python
# Calculate RSI
def calculate_rsi(data, window=14):
delta = data['Close'].diff()
gain = (delta.where(delta > 0, 0)).rolling(window=window).mean() loss = (-delta.where(delta < 0, 0)).rolling(window=window).mean()
rs = gain / loss
rsi = 100 - (100 / (1 + rs))return rsi
data['RSI'] = calculate_rsi(data) # Calculate Stochastic Oscillator
def calculate_stochastic(data, k=14, d=3):
low_min = data['Low'].rolling(window=k).min()
high_max = data['High'].rolling(window=k).max()
data['%K'] = ((
```

Chapter 10: Machine Learning for Trading with python – scripts

Machine learning has revolutionized the world of trading by enabling traders to make more informed decisions based on data analysis and pattern recognition. Python, with its powerful libraries such as NumPy, pandas, and scikit-learn, has become the preferred language for implementing machine learning algorithms in trading.

In this article, we will explore how to use Python scripts to implement machine learning for trading. We will cover basic concepts, data preprocessing, model training, and evaluation using real-world examples.

Basic Concepts:

Machine learning involves training a model on historical data to make predictions on future data. In trading, this means using past price movements, volume, and other market indicators to predict future price movements.

There are two main types of machine learning algorithms used in trading: supervised learning and unsupervised learning. Supervised learning involves training a model on labeled data, where the target variable (e.g. price movement) is known. Unsupervised learning involves finding patterns in unlabeled data.

Data Preprocessing:

Before training a machine learning model, it is important to preprocess the data to make it suitable for the algorithm. This involves cleaning the data, handling missing values, and normalizing the features.

For example, let's say we have a dataset of stock prices with columns for open, high, low, close prices, and volume. We can use Python scripts to clean the data, fill in missing values, and scale the features using the MinMaxScaler from scikit-learn.

Model Training:

Once the data is preprocessed, we can train a machine learning model using Python scripts. In this example, we will use a simple linear regression model to predict stock prices based on historical data.

First, we split the data into training and testing sets using train_test_split from scikit-learn. Then, we create a linear regression model using LinearRegression from scikit-learn and fit it to the training data.

```python
from sklearn.model_selection import train_test_split
from sklearn.linear_model import LinearRegression
from sklearn.preprocessing import MinMaxScaler

# Preprocess the data
# Fill missing values, scale the features
# Split the data into training and testing sets
X_train, X_test, y_train, y_test = train_test_split(X, y, test_size=0.2, random_state=42)
```

```python
# Create a linear regression model model = LinearRegression()

# Fit the model to the training data model.fit(X_train, y_train)
```

Model Evaluation:

After training the model, we can evaluate its performance using Python scripts. We can calculate metrics such as mean squared error, mean absolute error, and R-squared to measure the model's accuracy.

```python
from sklearn.metrics import mean_squared_error, mean_absolute_error, r2_score

# Make predictions on the testing data y_pred = model.predict(X_test)

# Calculate metrics
mse = mean_squared_error(y_test, y_pred) mae = mean_absolute_error(y_test, y_pred) r2 = r2_score(y_test, y_pred)

print("Mean Squared Error:", mse) print("Mean Absolute Error:", mae)print("R-squared:", r2)
```

Real-World Example:

Let's apply machine learning to a real-world trading scenario. We will use historical stock price data for Apple (AAPL) and train a model to predict future price movements.

First, we need to download the historical stock price data using a Python library such as yfinance.

```python
import yfinance as yf

# Download historical stock price data for AAPL
data = yf.download('AAPL', start='2020-01-01', end='2021-01-01')
```

Next, we preprocess the data by selecting the relevant features and scaling the data.

```python
# Select the relevant features
X = data[['Open', 'High', 'Low', 'Volume']]y = data['Close']

# Scale the features scaler = MinMaxScaler()
X_scaled = scaler.fit_transform(X)
```

Then, we split the data into training and testing sets and train a linear regression model.

```python
```

```python
# Split the data into training and testing sets
X_train, X_test, y_train, y_test = train_test_split(X_scaled, y, test_size=0.2, random_state=42)

# Create a linear regression model model = LinearRegression()

# Fit the model to the training data model.fit(X_train, y_train)
```

Finally, we evaluate the model's performance and make predictions on future data.

```python
# Make predictions on the testing data y_pred = model.predict(X_test)

# Calculate metrics
mse = mean_squared_error(y_test, y_pred) mae = mean_absolute_error(y_test, y_pred) r2 = r2_score(y_test, y_pred)

print("Mean Squared Error:", mse) print("Mean Absolute Error:",
```

Machine Learning Techniques for Trading Strategy

Machine learning techniques have revolutionized the way trading strategies are developed and implemented in the financial markets. By leveraging the power of algorithms and data analysis, traders can now make more informed decisions and improve their overall performance. In this article, we will explore some of the most widely used machine learning techniques for trading strategies and how they can be applied to achieve better results.

One of the key advantages of using machine learning techniques in trading is the ability to analyze large amounts of data quickly and accurately. Traditional trading strategies often rely on human intuition and experience, which can be limited by cognitive biases and emotions. Machine learning algorithms, on the other hand, can process vast amounts of data in real-time and identify patterns and trends that may not be apparent to human traders.

One of the most popular machine learning techniques used in trading strategies is supervised learning. In supervised learning, the algorithm is trained on historical data with known outcomes to predict future price movements. For example, a trader may use historical price data and technical indicators to train a machine learning model to predict whether a stock will go up or down in the next trading session.

Another commonly used machine learning technique in

trading strategies is reinforcement learning. In reinforcement learning, the algorithm learns through trial and error by receiving feedback on its actions. Traders can use reinforcement learning algorithms to optimize their trading strategies by maximizing profits and minimizing losses over time.

One of the key challenges in applying machine learning techniques to trading strategies is the need for high-quality data. Traders must ensure that the data used to train their machine learning models is accurate, up-to-date, and relevant to the markets they are trading in. Additionally, traders must be mindful of overfitting, where a model performs well on historical data but fails to generalize to new data.

Despite these challenges, machine learning techniques have been shown to outperform traditional trading strategies in many cases. By leveraging the power of algorithms and data analysis, traders can make more informed decisions and improve their overall performance in the financial markets.

One of the key benefits of using machine learning techniques in trading strategies is the ability to automate the decision-making process. By developing machine learning models that can analyze data and make predictions in real-time, traders can execute trades faster and more efficiently than ever before. This can give traders a competitive edge in fast-paced markets where speed is essential.

In addition to speed, machine learning techniques can

also help traders identify new trading opportunities that may not be apparent through traditional analysis methods. By analyzing large amounts of data and identifying patterns and trends, machine learning algorithms can uncover hidden opportunities for profit that may have beenoverlooked by human traders.

Machine learning techniques can also help traders manage risk more effectively. By analyzing historical data and identifying potential risks, traders can develop strategies to mitigate losses and protect their investments. For example, machine learning algorithms can be used to identify market conditions that are likely to result in losses and adjust trading strategies accordingly.

Overall, machine learning techniques have the potential to revolutionize the way trading strategies are developedand implemented in the financial markets. By leveraging the power of algorithms and data analysis, traders can make more informed decisions, automate the decision-making process, identify new trading opportunities, and manage risk more effectively. As technology continues to advance, we can expect to see even more innovative machine learning techniques being applied to trading strategies in the future.

Applying Machine Learning to Market Data with Python - Scripts

Applying machine learning to market data is a powerful way to gain insights and make informed decisions in the financial markets. By using Python scripts, we can leverage the capabilities of machine learning algorithms to analyze and predict market trends, identify trading opportunities, and optimize investment strategies.

In this article, we will explore how to apply machine learning to market data using Python scripts. We will cover the basics of machine learning, how to prepare market data for analysis, and provide examples of Python scripts for implementing machine learning algorithms.

Machine learning is a subset of artificial intelligence that enables computers to learn from data and make predictions or decisions without being explicitly programmed. In the context of financial markets, machine learning can be used to analyze historical market data, identify patterns and trends, and make predictions about future market movements.

To apply machine learning to market data, we first need to prepare the data for analysis. This involves collecting historical market data from sources such as financial websites or APIs, cleaning and preprocessing the data to remove any outliers or missing values, and splitting the data into training and testing sets.

Once the data is prepared, we can start building machine

learning models using Python. Python is a popular programming language for data analysis and machine learning, thanks to its rich ecosystem of libraries such as NumPy, pandas, and scikit-learn.

One common machine learning algorithm used in financial markets is the linear regression model. This model is used to predict the value of a dependent variable based on one or more independent variables. In the context of market data, we can use linear regression to predict the price of a stock based on historical price data and other relevant factors.

Below is an example of a Python script that implements a simple linear regression model to predict the price of a stock based on historical market data:

```python
import numpy as np import pandas as pd
from sklearn.linear_model import LinearRegression from sklearn.model_selection import train_test_split

# Load historical market data
data = pd.read_csv('market_data.csv')

# Prepare the data
X = data[['Volume', 'Open', 'High', 'Low']].values y = data['Close'].values

# Split the data into training and testing sets
X_train, X_test, y_train, y_test = train_test_split(X, y, test_size=0.2, random_state=0)
```

```
# Build and train the linear regression model model =
LinearRegression() model.fit(X_train, y_train)

# Make predictions
predictions = model.predict(X_test)

# Evaluate the model
accuracy = model.score(X_test, y_test) print(f'Accuracy:
{accuracy}')
```

In this script, we first load historical market data from a
CSV file using the pandas library. We then prepare the data
by selecting relevant features (Volume, Open, High, Low)
as independent variables and the closing price as the
dependent variable. We split the data into training and
testing sets using the train_test_split function from scikit-
learn.

Next, we build a linear regression model using the
LinearRegression class from scikit-learn and train the
model on the training data. We then use the model to
make predictions on the testing data and evaluate the
model's accuracy using the score method.

This is just a simple example of how machine learning can
be applied to market data using Python. There are many
other machine learning algorithms that can be used for
more complex analysis, such as decision trees, random
forests, and neural networks.

In addition to predicting stock prices, machine learning

can also be used for other tasks such as sentiment analysis of news articles, portfolio optimization, and risk management. By leveraging the power of machine learning, traders and investors can gain a competitive edge in the financial markets.

Applying machine learning to market data with Python scripts is a powerful way to analyze and predict market trends, identify trading opportunities, and optimize investment strategies. Python's rich ecosystem of libraries makes it easy to implement machine learning algorithms and analyze market data effectively. By combining machine learning with market data, traders and investors can make more informed decisions and achieve better results in the financial markets.

Chapter 11: Risk Management Strategies Trading System

Risk management is a crucial aspect of any trading system. Without proper risk management strategies in place, traders are exposed to significant financial losses that can potentially wipe out their entire trading capital. In this chapter, we will discuss some key risk management strategies that traders can implement to protect their investments and minimize potential losses.

Setting Stop Loss Orders

One of the most basic risk management strategies in trading is setting stop loss orders. A stop loss order is a predetermined price level at which a trader will exit a trade to limit their losses. By setting stop loss orders, traders can protect themselves from large losses in case the market moves against their position. It is important to set stop loss orders at a level that is based on the trader's risk tolerance and trading strategy.

Diversification

Diversification is another important risk management strategy that traders can use to spread their risk across different assets or markets. By diversifying their portfolio, traders can reduce the impact of a single trade or market event on their overall investment. Diversification can be achieved by trading different asset classes, such as stocks, bonds, commodities, and currencies, or by trading in different markets, such as equities, futures, and options.

Position Sizing

Position sizing is a risk management strategy that involves determining the amount of capital to allocate to each trade based on the trader's risk tolerance and trading strategy. By properly sizing their positions, traders can limit their exposure to potential losses and protect their trading capital. Position sizing can be calculated using various methods, such as the fixed dollar amount method, the percentage risk method, or the volatility-based method.

Risk-Reward Ratio

The risk-reward ratio is a key risk management metric that traders can use to assess the potential profitability of a trade relative to its risk. By calculating the risk-reward ratio before entering a trade, traders can determine whether the potential reward justifies the risk of the trade. A good risk-reward ratio is typically at least 1:2, meaning that the potential reward is at least twice the size of the potential risk.

Risk Limits

Setting risk limits is an important risk management strategy that traders can use to define their maximum acceptable loss per trade or per day. By setting risk limits, traders can prevent emotional decision-making and avoid chasing losses. Risk limits can be set based on the trader's risk tolerance, trading strategy, and overall financial goals.

Regular Monitoring and Evaluation

Risk management is an ongoing process that requires regular monitoring and evaluation of the trading system.

Traders should regularly review their trading performance, risk exposure, and risk management strategies to identify any weaknesses or areas for improvement. By continuously monitoring and evaluating their trading system, traders can adapt to changing market conditions and improve their overall risk management practices.

Risk management is a critical component of any trading system. By implementing proper risk management strategies, traders can protect their investments, minimize potential losses, and improve their overall trading performance.

The risk management strategies discussed in this chapter, such as setting stop loss orders, diversification, position sizing, risk-reward ratio, risk limits, and regular monitoring and evaluation, can help traders navigate the complex and volatile world of financial markets with confidence and success.

Importance of Risk Management in Trading Strategy

Risk management is a crucial aspect of any trading strategy, as it helps traders protect their capital and minimizepotential losses. In the volatile world of trading, where prices can fluctuate rapidly and unexpectedly, having a solid risk management plan in place is essential for long-term success.

One of the key reasons why risk management is important in trading is that it helps traders avoid large losses thatcan wipe out their capital. By setting strict risk limits and using stop-loss orders, traders can ensure that they will not lose more than a predetermined amount on any single trade. This helps to protect their capital and allows them to continue trading even after a series of losing trades.

In addition to protecting capital, risk management also helps traders stay disciplined and avoid emotional decision-making. When traders are faced with the prospect of losing money, they may be tempted to abandon their trading strategy and make impulsive decisions in an attempt to recoup their losses. However, a well-defined risk management plan can help traders stay focused on their long-term goals and avoid making costly mistakes.

Furthermore, risk management can also help traders maximize their profits by allowing them to take calculated risks. By carefully assessing the potential risks and rewards of each trade, traders can make informed decisions that have the potential to generate significant returns. This can help traders achieve their financial goals and grow their trading account over time.

Another important aspect of risk management in trading is diversification. By spreading their capital across a variety of assets and markets, traders can reduce their exposure to any single risk factor and minimize the impact of unexpected events. Diversification can help traders manage their risk more effectively and ensure that their trading strategy remains robust in the face of changing market conditions.

Risk management also plays a crucial role in helping traders build confidence in their trading strategy. By knowing that they have a solid risk management plan in place, traders can trade with more conviction and avoid second-guessing their decisions. This can help traders stay focused on their trading goals and maintain a positive mindset, even during challenging market conditions.

In conclusion, risk management is an essential component of any trading strategy. By protecting capital, minimizing losses, staying disciplined, maximizing profits, diversifying risk, and building confidence, risk management can help traders achieve long-term success in the competitive world of trading. Traders who prioritize risk management are more likely to weather market fluctuations, stay profitable, and achieve their financial goals over time.

Implementing Stop-Loss and Take-Profit with python - scripts

In the world of trading, implementing stop-loss and take-profit orders is essential for managing risk and maximizing profits. These orders are used to automatically close a trade at a predetermined price level, protecting traders from large losses and locking in profits when the market moves in their favor. In this article, we will explore how to implement stop-loss and take-profit orders using Python scripts.

Stop-Loss Order

A stop-loss order is a type of order that is placed to limit the amount of loss that a trader is willing to take on a trade. When the market reaches the stop-loss price level, the trade is automatically closed at that price, preventing further losses. Stop-loss orders are crucial for risk management and protecting capital in volatile markets.

To implement a stop-loss order in Python, we can use the popular trading library called `ccxt`. This library provides a unified API for accessing various cryptocurrency exchanges and executing trades. Here is an example of how to implement a stop-loss order using `ccxt`:

```python
import ccxt

# Initialize the exchange exchange = ccxt.binance({
'apiKey': 'YOUR_API_KEY', 'secret': 'YOUR_API_SECRET',
```

```
})

# Get the current price of the assetsymbol = 'BTC/USDT'
price = exchange.fetch_ticker(symbol)['last']

# Set the stop-loss price level stop_loss_price = price *
0.95

# Place the stop-loss order
order = exchange.create_order(symbol, 'market', 'sell',
0.01, stop_loss_price, {'stopPrice': stop_loss_price,
})
```

In this script, we first initialize the `ccxt` exchange object with our API key and secret. We then fetch the current price of the asset we want to trade and calculate the stop-loss price level, which is set at 5% below the current price. Finally, we place a market sell order with a stop-price parameter, which triggers the order when the market price reaches the stop-loss price level.

Take-Profit Order

A take-profit order is a type of order that is placed to lock in profits when the market moves in the trader's favor. When the market reaches the take-profit price level, the trade is automatically closed at that price, ensuring that the trader does not miss out on potential profits. Take-profit orders are essential for maximizing profits and capitalizing on favorable market movements.

To implement a take-profit order in Python, we can use the same `ccxt` library as before. Here is an example of how to implement a take-profit order using `ccxt`:

```python
import ccxt

# Initialize the exchange exchange = ccxt.binance({
'apiKey': 'YOUR_API_KEY', 'secret': 'YOUR_API_SECRET',
})

# Get the current price of the assetsymbol = 'BTC/USDT'
price = exchange.fetch_ticker(symbol)['last']

# Set the take-profit price level take_profit_price = price * 1.05

# Place the take-profit order
order = exchange.create_order(symbol, 'market', 'sell', 0.01, take_profit_price, {'stopPrice': take_profit_price,
})
```

In this script, we again initialize the `ccxt` exchange object with our API key and secret. We fetch the current price of the asset and calculate the take-profit price level, which is set at 5% above the current price. We then place a market sell order with a stop-price parameter, which triggers the order when the market price reaches the take-profit price level.

Combining Stop-Loss and Take-Profit Orders

To effectively manage risk and maximize profits, traders often use a combination of stop-loss and take-profit orders in their trading strategies. By implementing both types of orders, traders can protect their capital from large losses while locking in profits when the market moves in their favor.

In Python, we can easily combine stop-loss and take-profit orders in a single script using the `ccxt` library. Here is an example of how to implement both orders simultaneously:

```python
import ccxt
```

```python
# Initialize the exchange exchange = ccxt.binance({
'apiKey':          'YOUR_API_KEY',          'secret':
'YOUR_API_SECRET',
})

# Get the current price of the assetsymbol = 'BTC/USDT'
price = exchange.fetch_ticker(symbol)['last']

# Set the stop-loss and take-profit price levels
stop_loss_price = price * 0.95 take_profit_price = price *
1.05

# Place the stop-loss order
stop_loss_order    =    exchange.create_order(symbol,
'market',  'sell',  0.01,  stop_loss_price,  {  'stopPrice':
stop_loss_price,
})

# Place the take-profit order
take_profit_order = exchange.create_order(symbol
```

Chapter 12: Optimizing Trading Strategies with python

In this chapter, we will explore how to optimize trading strategies using Python. Optimization is a crucial step in the development of trading strategies as it helps to improve the performance of the strategy by fine-tuning its parameters. By optimizing trading strategies, traders can maximize their profits and reduce their risks.

There are several ways to optimize trading strategies in Python. One common approach is to use an optimization algorithm to search for the best set of parameters that maximize a certain performance metric, such as profit or Sharpe ratio. In this chapter, we will focus on using the popular optimization library, scipy.optimize, to optimize trading strategies.

To start optimizing a trading strategy, we first need to define the objective function that we want to optimize. This function should take the parameters of the trading strategy as inputs and return a performance metric that we want to maximize or minimize. For example, if we want to maximize the profit of a trading strategy, the objective function could be defined as the total profit generated by the strategy.

Next, we need to define the parameter space that we want to search for the optimal parameters. This can be done by specifying the range of values for each parameter that we want to optimize. For example, if we want to optimize the moving average crossover strategy, we can specify the range of values for the short and long moving average periods.

Once we have defined the objective function and parameter space, we can use the scipy.optimize library to search for the optimal parameters. One common optimization algorithm that is used for this purpose is the Nelder-Mead algorithm, which is a derivative-free optimization algorithm that is suitable for optimizing non-linear functions.

To use the Nelder-Mead algorithm for optimizing trading strategies, we first need to import the optimize module from the scipy library. We can then define the objective function and parameter space as described earlier.
Finally, we can call the minimize function from the optimize module with the objective function and parameter space as arguments to search for the optimal parameters.

In addition to the Nelder-Mead algorithm, there are several other optimization algorithms that can be used to optimize trading strategies in Python. Some popular optimization algorithms include the genetic algorithm, particle swarm optimization, and simulated annealing. These algorithms can be used to search for the optimal parameters of trading strategies in a more efficient manner.

In conclusion, optimizing trading strategies is a crucial step in the development of profitable trading strategies. By using Python and optimization algorithms, traders can

131

fine-tune their strategies to maximize their profits and reduce their risks. In this chapter, we have discussed how to optimize trading strategies using the scipy.optimize library in Python. By following the steps outlined in this chapter, traders can improve the performance of their trading strategies and achieve better results in the financial markets.

Techniques for Optimization Trading System with Python - Scripts

Optimization trading systems are essential tools for traders looking to maximize their profits and minimize risks in the financial markets. These systems use mathematical algorithms and statistical models to analyze market data and make informed trading decisions. Python is a popular programming language for developing optimization trading systems due to its simplicity, flexibility, and extensive libraries for data analysis and visualization.

We will explore some techniques for optimizing trading systems using Python scripts. We will provide examples of how to implement these techniques in Python code to build a robust and efficient trading system.

Backtesting

Backtesting is a crucial step in optimizing trading systems as it allows traders to evaluate the performance of their strategies using historical market data. Python provides several libraries such as Pandas and Matplotlib that make it easy to backtest trading strategies and visualize the results.

Here is an example of a simple backtesting script in Python:

```python
import pandas as pd
```

```python
import matplotlib.pyplot as plt

# Load historical market data
data = pd.read_csv('historical_data.csv')

# Calculate moving averages
data['MA50'] = data['Close'].rolling(window=50).mean()
data['MA200']                                       =
data['Close'].rolling(window=200).mean()

# Generate trading signalsdata['Signal'] = 0
data['Signal'][data['MA50'] > data['MA200']] = 1
data['Signal'][data['MA50'] < data['MA200']] = -1

# Calculate returns
data['Returns']       =       data['Close'].pct_change()       *
data['Signal'].shift(1)

#       Plot       results       plt.figure(figsize=(10,       5))
plt.plot(data['Close'])
plt.plot(data['MA50'])
plt.plot(data['MA200'])       plt.legend(['Close',       'MA50',
'MA200'])plt.show()
```

This script demonstrates how to backtest a simple moving average crossover strategy using historical market data. It calculates the moving averages of the closing prices, generates trading signals based on the crossover of the moving averages, and calculates the returns of the strategy.

Parameter Optimization

Parameter optimization involves finding the optimal values for the parameters of a trading strategy to maximize its performance. Python provides libraries such as Scikit-learn and Optuna that can be used to automate the process of parameter optimization.

Here is an example of a parameter optimization script in Python using Optuna:

```python
import optuna

def objective(trial):
# Define parameters to optimize
param1 = trial.suggest_int('param1', 1, 10)
param2 = trial.suggest_float('param2', 0.1, 1.0)

# Calculate performance metricscore = param1 * param2

return score

study = optuna.create_study(direction='maximize')
study.optimize(objective, n_trials=100)

best_params = study.best_params best_score =
```

```
study.best_value

print('Best parameters:', best_params)print('Best score:',
best_score)
```
```
```

This script demonstrates how to use Optuna to optimize the parameters of a trading strategy. It defines the parameters to optimize, calculates a performance metric based on the parameters, and finds the optimal valuesfor the parameters that maximize the performance metric.

Portfolio Optimization

Portfolio optimization involves selecting the optimal allocation of assets in a portfolio to maximize returns and minimize risks. Python provides libraries such as PyPortfolioOpt and cvxopt that can be used to optimize portfolio allocations.

Here is an example of a portfolio optimization script in Python using PyPortfolioOpt:

```python
from pypfopt.efficient_frontier import EfficientFrontier
from pypfopt import risk_models
from pypfopt import expected_returns

# Load historical market data
data = pd.read_csv('historical_data.csv')

# Calculate expected returns and covariance matrix mu =
expected_returns.mean_historical_return(data)    S    =
risk_models.sample_cov(data)

# Optimize portfolio allocation ef = EfficientFrontier(mu,
S) weights = ef.max_sharpe()

print('Optimal portfolio allocation:')print(weights)
```

This script demonstrates how to use PyPortfolioOpt to
optimize the allocation of assets in a portfolio. It
calculates the expected returns and covariance matrix of
the assets, constructs an efficient frontier based on the
returns and risks of the assets, and finds the optimal
allocation of assets that maximizes the Sharpe ratio.

Optimization trading systems play a crucial role in helping
traders make informed decisions and maximize their
profits in the financial markets. Python provides a
powerful platform for developing and implementing
optimization trading systems due to its simplicity,
flexibility, and extensive libraries for data analysis and
visualization.

By using techniques such as backtesting, parameter optimization, and portfolio optimization, traders can build robust and efficient trading systems that can adapt to changing market conditions and achieve their financial goals.

Performance Metrics and Analysis trading with python - scripts

Performance metrics and analysis are crucial components of successful trading strategies. By measuring and analyzing the performance of your trades, you can identify strengths and weaknesses in your strategy, make informed decisions, and ultimately improve your trading results. In this article, we will explore the concept of performance metrics and analysis in trading, and provide examples of how to implement them using Python scripts.

Performance Metrics in Trading

Performance metrics are quantitative measures that assess the effectiveness of a trading strategy. These metrics provide valuable insights into the profitability, risk, and overall performance of your trades. By analyzing these metrics, you can track your progress, identify areas for improvement, and make informed decisions to optimize your trading strategy.

Some common performance metrics used in trading include:

Return on Investment (ROI): ROI measures the profitability of your trades relative to the capital invested. It is calculated as the net profit divided by the initial investment, expressed as a percentage.

Sharpe Ratio: The Sharpe Ratio measures the risk-adjusted return of a trading strategy. It takes into account both the return and the volatility of the strategy, providing a more comprehensive measure of performance.

Maximum Drawdown: Maximum drawdown measures the largest peak-to-trough decline in the value of your trading account. It indicates the maximum loss incurred by the strategy during a specific period.

Win Rate: Win rate measures the percentage of winning trades relative to the total number of trades. A high win rate indicates a successful trading strategy, while a low win rate may signify inefficiencies in the strategy.

Average Profit/Loss: Average profit/loss measures the average gain or loss per trade. It provides insights into the profitability of individual trades and helps identify patterns in the trading strategy.

Implementing Performance Metrics Analysis in Python

Python is a powerful programming language commonly used in quantitative finance and algorithmic trading. With its extensive libraries and tools, Python provides a flexible and efficient platform for analyzing trading performance metrics. Below are examples of Python scripts that demonstrate how to implement performance metrics analysis in trading.

Calculating Return on Investment (ROI)

To calculate the ROI of a trading strategy, you can use the following Python script:

```python
def calculate_roi(profit, capital): return (profit / capital) * 100


# Example:
profit = 1000
capital = 5000
roi = calculate_roi(profit, capital) print("ROI: {}%".format(roi))
```

In this script, the `calculate_roi` function takes the profit and initial capital as input parameters and calculates the ROI as a percentage. The example demonstrates how to calculate the ROI for a profit of $1000 and initial capital of $5000.

Computing Sharpe Ratio

To compute the Sharpe Ratio of a trading strategy, you can use the following Python script:

```python
import numpy as np

def calculate_sharpe_ratio(returns, risk_free_rate):
    mean_return = np.mean(returns) std_dev = np.std(returns)
    return (mean_return - risk_free_rate) / std_dev

# Example:
returns = [0.02, 0.03, 0.01, 0.05, 0.02]
```

```python
risk_free_rate = 0.01
sharpe_ratio   =   calculate_sharpe_ratio(returns,
risk_free_rate)          print("Sharpe          Ratio:
{}".format(sharpe_ratio))
```

In this script, the `calculate_sharpe_ratio` function takes
a list of returns and the risk-free rate as input parameters
and computes the Sharpe Ratio. The example
demonstrates how to calculate the Sharpe Ratio for a list of
returns and a risk-free rate of 1%.

Analyzing Maximum Drawdown

To analyze the maximum drawdown of a trading strategy,
you can use the following Python script:

```python
def calculate_max_drawdown(returns): peak = 0
drawdown = 0
max_drawdown = 0

for ret in returns:
peak = max(peak, ret) drawdown = (peak - ret) / peak


max_drawdown  =  max(max_drawdown,  drawdown) return
max_drawdown
# Example:
returns = [0.02, -0.05, 0.03, -0.02, 0.01]
max_drawdown  =  calculate_max_drawdown(returns)
print("Maximum  Drawdown:  {}".format(max_drawdown))
```

In this script, the `calculate_max_drawdown` function takes a list of returns as input and calculates the maximum drawdown. The example demonstrates how to calculate the maximum drawdown for a list of returns.

Evaluating Win Rate

To evaluate the win rate of a trading strategy, you can use the following Python script:

```python
def calculate_win_rate(trades):total_trades = len(trades)
winning_tr
```

Chapter 13: Automating Trade Execution with python

In the world of trading, speed is of the essence. Traders are constantly looking for ways to automate their trade execution in order to gain an edge in the market. One of the most popular tools for automating trade execution is Python, a powerful and versatile programming language that is widely used in the financial industry.

In this chapter, we will explore how Python can be used to automate trade execution and streamline the trading process. We will cover the basics of using Python for trade execution, including how to connect to a trading platform, place trades, and manage risk. We will also discuss some best practices for automating trade execution with Python, as well as some common pitfalls to avoid.

Connecting to a Trading Platform

The first step in automating trade execution with Python is to connect to a trading platform. There are many different trading platforms available, each with its own API for connecting to and interacting with the platform. Some popular trading platforms that offer APIs for Python include Interactive Brokers, TD Ameritrade, and Alpaca.

To connect to a trading platform using Python, you will need to install the appropriate API library for the platform you are using. Once you have installed the API library, you can use Python to connect to the platform, authenticate your account, and access the platform's trading functions.

Placing Trades

Once you have connected to a trading platform, you can use Python to place trades automatically. This can be done by writing a script that specifies the parameters of the trade, such as the symbol, quantity, and order type. You can then use the API functions provided by the trading platform to execute the trade.

When placing trades automatically with Python, it is important to consider factors such as slippage, liquidity, and market conditions. It is also important to implement risk management strategies to protect your capital and minimize losses.

Managing Risk

Risk management is a crucial aspect of automated trade execution. When automating trade execution with Python, it is important to implement risk management strategies to protect your capital and minimize losses. This can be done by setting stop-loss orders, implementing position sizing rules, and monitoring your trades closely.

It is also important to backtest your trading strategies before implementing them in a live trading environment. This can help you identify potential weaknesses in your strategy and make adjustments before risking real capital.

Best Practices for Automating Trade Execution with Python

When automating trade execution with Python, there are some best practices to keep in mind. These include:

Testing your code thoroughly before deploying it in a live trading environment.
Implementing risk management strategies to protect your capital.
Monitoring your trades closely and making adjustments as needed.
Keeping your code clean and organized to make it easier to maintain and debug.

Common Pitfalls to Avoid

There are also some common pitfalls to avoid when automating trade execution with Python. These include:

Over-optimizing your trading strategy based on historical data.

Failing to implement proper risk management strategies.

Ignoring market conditions and blindly following a trading strategy.

Failing to monitor your trades closely and make adjustments as needed.

Automating trade execution with Python can help traders gain an edge in the market by streamlining the trading process and allowing for faster execution of trades. By following best practices and avoiding common pitfalls, traders can use Python to automate their trade execution effectively and efficiently.

Connecting to Exchanges Trading System with python - scripts

Connecting to exchanges trading system with Python can be a powerful tool for traders looking to automate their trading strategies. By using Python scripts, traders can connect to various exchanges, access real-time market data, place trades, and manage their portfolios all from the comfort of their own computer.

To get started with connecting to an exchanges trading system with Python, you will need to have a basic understanding of Python programming language and some knowledge of how trading systems work. In this article, we will provide an example of how to connect to a popular exchange using Python scripts.

First, you will need to install the necessary libraries to connect to the exchange. One of the most popular libraries for connecting to exchanges in Python is the ccxt library. This library provides a unified API for connecting to over 100 different cryptocurrency exchanges.

To install the ccxt library, you can use pip, the Python package manager. Simply open a terminal window and type the following command:

```bash
pip install ccxt
```

Once you have installed the ccxt library, you can start

writing your Python script to connect to the exchange. In this example, we will connect to the Binance exchange, one of the largest cryptocurrency exchanges in the world.

```python
import ccxt

# Create an instance of the Binance exchange
exchange = ccxt.binance({
'apiKey': 'YOUR_API_KEY',
'secret': 'YOUR_API_SECRET'
})

# Fetch the current balance of your account
balance = exchange.fetch_balance()

print(balance)
```

In this script, we first import the ccxt library and create an instance of the Binance exchange using our API key and secret. We then fetch the current balance of our account using the `fetch_balance()` method provided by the ccxt library.

Once you have connected to the exchange and fetched your account balance, you can start implementing your trading strategy. For example, you can fetch real-time market data, place buy or sell orders, and manage your portfolio all within your Python script.

```python
# Fetch the current price of Bitcoin
btc_price = exchange.fetch_ticker('BTC/USDT')['last']
print(f"The current price of Bitcoin is {btc_price}")
# Place a buy order for 0.1 Bitcoin at the current price
order = exchange.create_order('BTC/USDT', 'limit', 'buy',
0.1, btc_price)

print(order)
```

In this example, we fetch the current price of Bitcoin against USDT and place a buy order for 0.1 Bitcoin at the current price. We then print the order details to the console.

Connecting to exchanges trading system with Python can be a powerful tool for traders looking to automate their trading strategies. By using Python scripts and the ccxt library, traders can connect to various exchanges, access real-time market data, place trades, and manage their portfolios all from the comfort of their own computer.

In addition to connecting to exchanges, Python scripts can also be used to analyze market data, implement trading algorithms, and backtest trading strategies. By combining Python with popular libraries such as Pandas, NumPy, and Matplotlib, traders can create sophisticated trading systems that can help them make better trading decisions.

Overall, connecting to exchanges trading system with Python can provide traders with a powerful tool to automate their trading strategies and make more informed trading decisions. By using Python scripts and the ccxt library, traders can connect to various exchanges, access real-time market data, place trades, and manage their portfolios all from the comfort of their own computer.

Executing Trades Programmatically Trading System with Python - scripts

Executing trades programmatically is a powerful tool for traders looking to automate their trading strategies. By writing scripts in a programming language such as Python, traders can execute trades based on predefined conditions without having to manually place each trade themselves. In this article, we will discuss how to create a trading system using Python scripts and walk through an example of executing trades programmatically.

Python is a popular programming language for building trading systems due to its simplicity and versatility. With libraries such as pandas, numpy, and matplotlib, traders can easily analyze market data, create trading signals, and execute trades. Additionally, Python's syntax is easy to learn and understand, making it an ideal choice for traders with varying levels of programming experience.

To begin building a trading system in Python, traders first need to define their trading strategy. This strategy could be based on technical indicators, fundamental analysis, or a combination of both. Once the trading strategy is defined, traders can start writing Python scripts to implement their strategy.

One of the key components of a trading system is the ability to execute trades based on predefined conditions. This can be achieved using an API provided by a brokerage or exchange. By connecting to the API using Python, traders can send buy and sell orders directly from their scripts.

In the following example, we will walk through a simple trading system that executes trades programmatically using Python scripts. This example will use the Alpaca API, a commission-free brokerage that provides a simple and easy-to-use API for trading stocks.

First, traders need to create an account with Alpaca and generate API keys. These API keys will be used to authenticate with the Alpaca API and execute trades. Once the API keys are generated, traders can start writing Python scripts to connect to the Alpaca API and place trades.

```python
import alpaca_trade_api as tradeapi # Define API keys
API_KEY = 'your_api_key'
API_SECRET = 'your_api_secret'
BASE_URL = 'https://paper-api.alpaca.markets'

# Connect to Alpaca API
api = tradeapi.REST(API_KEY, API_SECRET, BASE_URL, api_version='v2')

# Get account information account = api.get_account()
print(account)
```

In this script, we first import the alpaca_trade_api library, which provides a Python interface to the Alpaca API. We then define our API keys and connect to the Alpaca API using the REST function. We can then use the get_account function to retrieve information about our account, such as our buying power and cash balance.

Next, we can define a simple trading strategy that buys a stock when the price crosses above a moving average and sells the stock when the price crosses below the moving average.

```
# Define trading strategy
def trading_strategy(symbol):
# Get historical data
bars = api.get_barset(symbol, 'day', limit=20)

# Calculate moving average
close_prices   =   [bar.c   for   bar   in   bars[symbol]]
moving_average  =  sum(close_prices)  /  len(close_prices)

# Get current price
current_price = api.get_last_trade(symbol).price

# Execute trade
if current_price > moving_average:
api.submit_order(symbol, 1, 'buy', 'market', 'gtc') elif
current_price < moving_average:
api.submit_order(symbol, 1, 'sell', 'market', 'gtc')
```

In this function, we first retrieve historical data for the specified stock using the get_barset function. We then calculate the moving average of the closing prices and get the current price of the stock. Based on the trading strategy, we submit a buy order if the current price is above the moving average and a sell order if the current price is below the moving average.

Finally, we can run our trading strategy on a list of stocks and execute trades based on the predefined conditions.# Define list of stocks

```
stocks = ['AAPL', 'MSFT', 'GOOGL']

# Execute trades for stock in stocks:
trading_strategy(stock)
```

By looping through a list of stocks and calling the trading_strategy function for each stock, we can execute trades programmatically based on our predefined conditions.

Executing trades programmatically using Python scripts is a powerful tool for traders looking to automate their trading strategies. By connecting to an API provided by a brokerage or exchange, traders can send buy and sell orders directly from their scripts. With Python's simplicity and versatility, traders can easily build and test trading systems to execute trades efficiently and effectively.

Chapter 14: High-Frequency Trading

High-frequency trading (HFT) is a type of trading that uses powerful computers to execute a large number of orders at extremely high speeds. This chapter will explore the ins and outs of high-frequency trading, including its history, benefits, risks, and impact on the financial markets.

History of High-Frequency Trading

High-frequency trading has been around for several decades, but it really took off in the early 2000s with the advent of electronic trading platforms and the proliferation of high-speed internet connections. In the past, traders would execute orders manually, but with the rise of HFT, computers now handle the majority of trading activity on the stock exchanges.

Benefits of High-Frequency Trading

One of the main benefits of high-frequency trading is its ability to provide liquidity to the markets. By executing a large number of orders at lightning-fast speeds, HFT firms help ensure that there are always buyers and sellers for every stock, which helps keep prices stable and prevents large price swings.

Another benefit of high-frequency trading is its ability to take advantage of small price discrepancies in the market. HFT firms use sophisticated algorithms to identify these discrepancies and profit from them by executing trades in milliseconds. This can result in significant profits for HFT firms, but it can also benefit other market participants by helping to keep prices in line with the true value of the underlying assets.

Risks of High-Frequency Trading

While high-frequency trading offers many benefits, it also comes with a number of risks. One of the main risks is the potential for market manipulation. HFT firms have the ability to move markets with their large trading volumes, and there have been instances where HFT firms have been accused of manipulating prices to their advantage.

Another risk of high-frequency trading is the potential for system failures. HFT firms rely on complex computer algorithms to execute their trades, and if these algorithms malfunction or encounter technical issues, it can lead to large losses for the firm and disruptions in the market.

Impact on the Financial Markets

High-frequency trading has had a profound impact on the financial markets. On the one hand, it has helped increase liquidity and reduce trading costs for investors. On the other hand, it has also been blamed for exacerbating market volatility and creating a two-tiered market where HFT firms have an advantage over traditional investors.

In recent years, regulators have taken steps to address some of the concerns surrounding high-frequency trading. For example, in 2010, the U.S. implemented a rule known as the "flash crash" rule, which requires HFT firms to have controls in place to prevent excessive volatility in the markets.

Overall, high-frequency trading is a complex and controversial topic that continues to evolve as technology advances and market dynamics change. While it offers many benefits, it also comes with risks that need to be carefully managed to ensure a fair and efficient financial system.

Fundamentals of HFT Trading

High-frequency trading (HFT) is a type of trading strategy that uses powerful computers to execute a large number of orders at extremely high speeds. This allows traders to take advantage of small price discrepancies and make profits in a matter of milliseconds. In this article, we will explore the fundamentals of HFT trading, including its history, strategies, and impact on the financial markets.

History of HFT Trading

HFT trading has its roots in the early 2000s when advancements in technology and the proliferation of electronic trading platforms made it possible for traders to execute orders at lightning-fast speeds. In the beginning, HFT was mainly used by large institutional investors and hedge funds to gain a competitive edge in the market.
However, as the technology became more accessible and affordable, HFT trading spread to retail traders and smaller firms.

Today, HFT trading accounts for a significant portion of the trading volume in major financial markets around the world. According to some estimates, HFT firms are responsible for up to 60% of all trades in the US stock market. This dominance has raised concerns about market manipulation and instability, leading regulators to introduce new rules and regulations to curb the impact of HFT on the markets.

Strategies Used in HFT Trading

HFT trading employs a variety of strategies to profit from small price discrepancies in the market. Some of the most common strategies used by HFT firms include:

Market Making: HFT firms act as market makers by continuously quoting bid and ask prices for a particular security. They profit from the spread between the bid and ask prices, which can be as small as a fraction of a penny. By providing liquidity to the market, HFT firms help ensure that there is always a buyer or seller for a security, which can reduce volatility and improve market efficiency.

Arbitrage: HFT firms use sophisticated algorithms to identify and exploit price discrepancies between different markets or securities. For example, they may buy a security on one exchange and sell it on another exchange where the price is slightly higher, pocketing the difference in price. Arbitrage opportunities are often short-lived, so HFT firms must act quickly to capitalize on them.

Momentum Trading: HFT firms use historical price data and technical indicators to identify trends and momentum in the market. They then place orders to take advantage of these trends, buying when prices are rising and selling when prices are falling. By reacting quickly to changing market conditions, HFT firms can profit from short-term price movements.

Impact of HFT Trading on the Financial Markets

The rise of HFT trading has had a profound impact on the financial markets, both positive and negative. Proponents of HFT argue that it has increased market liquidity, reduced trading costs, and improved price discovery.

By providing liquidity to the market, HFT firms help ensure that there is always a buyer or seller for a security, which can reduce volatility and improve market efficiency. Additionally, HFT firms compete with each other to offer the best prices, which can result in tighter bid-ask spreads for investors.

However, critics of HFT argue that it has also introduced new risks and challenges to the financial markets. One of the main concerns is that HFT firms may engage in manipulative trading practices, such as quote stuffing or spoofing, to distort prices and gain an unfair advantage over other market participants. Regulators have taken steps to address these concerns by implementing new rules and regulations to increase transparency and oversight of HFT trading activities.

In addition, HFT trading has been blamed for exacerbating market volatility and contributing to flash crashes, such as the one that occurred in the US stock market in 2010. During a flash crash, prices can plummet or spike dramatically in a matter of minutes, leading to widespread panic and confusion among investors. While HFT firms are not solely responsible for flash crashes, their high-speed trading activities can amplify market movements and make it difficult for regulators to intervene in a timely manner.

Despite these challenges, HFT trading continues to play a significant role in the financial markets and is likely to remain a key driver of market liquidity and efficiency in the future. As technology continues to advance and trading speeds increase, HFT firms will need to adapt and innovate to stay competitive in an increasingly complex and competitive market environment.

HFT trading is a sophisticated and high-risk trading strategy that relies on powerful computers and algorithms to execute orders at lightning-fast speeds. While HFT firms have revolutionized the way financial markets operate, they have also introduced new risks and challenges that regulators must address to ensure the stability and integrity of the markets.

Building High-Frequency Trading Systems with python

High-frequency trading (HFT) is a type of algorithmic trading that involves the use of powerful computers to execute trades at extremely fast speeds. These systems are designed to take advantage of small price discrepancies in the market and make quick profits. Python has become a popular programming language for building high-frequency trading systems due to its simplicity, flexibility, and powerful libraries.

In this article, we will discuss the basics of building high-frequency trading systems with Python. We will cover the key components of a high-frequency trading system, such as data acquisition, strategy development, order execution, and risk management. We will also provide some tips and best practices for building efficient and reliable high-frequency trading systems.

Data Acquisition

The first step in building a high-frequency trading system is to acquire market data. This data includes real-time price quotes, order book data, trade data, and other relevant information. There are several ways to access market data, such as using APIs provided by exchanges, data vendors, or third-party providers.

Python provides several libraries for accessing market data, such as pandas, numpy, and matplotlib. These libraries can be used to collect, clean, and analyze market data in real-time. For example, you can use the pandas library to read and process data from CSV files or APIs, and the matplotlib library to visualize market data in charts and graphs.

Strategy Development

Once you have acquired market data, the next step is to develop trading strategies. A trading strategy is a set of rules and conditions that determine when to buy or sell assets. High-frequency trading strategies are typically based on technical indicators, statistical models, machine learning algorithms, or a combination of these methods.

Python provides several libraries for developing trading strategies, such as numpy, scipy, and scikit-learn. These libraries can be used to implement complex mathematical models, backtest trading strategies, and optimize trading parameters. For example, you can use the scipy library to perform statistical analysis on market data, and the scikit-learn library to train machine learning models for predicting market movements.

Order Execution

Once you have developed trading strategies, the next step is to execute trades in the market. High-frequency trading systems are designed to execute trades at extremely fast speeds, often in milliseconds or microseconds. This requires a reliable and low-latency connection to the exchange, as well as efficient order routing algorithms.

Python provides several libraries for order execution, such

as asyncio, requests, and websockets. These libraries can be used to send orders to the exchange, receive order confirmations, and monitor order status in real-time. For example, you can use the asyncio library to create asynchronous tasks for sending orders, and the requests library to interact with exchange APIs.

Risk Management

Risk management is an important aspect of high-frequency trading systems. These systems are exposed to various risks, such as market risk, execution risk, and technology risk. It is important to implement risk management controls to protect the system from unexpected losses and ensure compliance with regulatory requirements.

Python provides several libraries for risk management, such as riskparity.py, pyfolio, and zipline. These libraries can be used to calculate risk metrics, monitor portfolio performance, and generate risk reports. For example, you can use the riskparity.py library to implement risk parity strategies, and the pyfolio library to analyze portfolio returns and risk-adjusted performance.

Tips and Best Practices

Here are some tips and best practices for building high-frequency trading systems with Python:

Use efficient data structures and algorithms to process market data in real-time.
Optimize code for performance and scalability to handle

high-frequency trading volumes.

Implement error handling and logging mechanisms to monitor system performance and troubleshoot issues.

Test trading strategies in a simulated environment before deploying them in the live market.

Stay up-to-date with the latest developments in high-frequency trading technology and regulations.

Building high-frequency trading systems with Python requires a solid understanding of market dynamics, trading strategies, order execution, and risk management. By following the tips and best practices outlined in this article, you can build efficient and reliable high-frequency trading systems that can generate profits in the fast-paced world of algorithmic trading.

Chapter 15: Ensuring Security in Automated Trading

Automated trading, also known as algorithmic trading, is a method of executing orders using pre-programmed instructions to trade in financial markets. This type of trading has become increasingly popular in recent years due to its ability to execute trades at high speeds and with minimal human intervention. However, with the rise of automated trading, concerns about security have also increased. In this chapter, we will discuss the importance of ensuring security in automated trading and the measures that can be taken to mitigate risks.

One of the main concerns with automated trading is the potential for cyber attacks. As automated trading systems rely on computers and networks to execute trades, they are vulnerable to hacking and other cyber threats. Hackers could potentially gain access to trading systems and manipulate trades for their own gain, leading to significant financial losses for traders and investors.

To mitigate the risk of cyber attacks, it is important for traders to implement robust security measures. This includes using encryption to protect sensitive data, implementing firewalls to prevent unauthorized access to trading systems, and regularly updating software to patch vulnerabilities. Traders should also monitor their systems for any suspicious activity and have protocols in place to respond quickly to any security breaches.

Another security concern with automated trading is the potential for system failures. If a trading system malfunctions or crashes, it could lead to significant financial losses for traders. To prevent system failures, traders should regularly test their automated trading systems and have backup systems in place to quickly resume trading in the event of a failure. Traders should also have contingency plans in place to manually execute trades if necessary.

Market manipulation is another security concern with automated trading. Traders could potentially manipulate markets by placing large orders to create artificial demand or supply, leading to price distortions. To prevent market manipulation, traders should adhere to regulations and best practices for automated trading. Traders should also monitor market activity closely and report any suspicious behavior to regulatory authorities.

In addition to external threats, traders should also be aware of internal threats to security in automated trading. Insider trading, where traders use non-public information to gain an unfair advantage in the market, is a significant concern. Traders should have strict policies in place to prevent insider trading, including monitoring employee trading activity and restricting access to sensitive information.

Overall, ensuring security in automated trading is essential to protect traders and investors from potential risks. By implementing robust security measures, monitoring trading systems for suspicious activity, and adhering to regulations and best practices, traders can mitigate the risks associated with automated trading. It is important for traders to stay informed about the latest security threats and take proactive steps to protect their trading systems. By prioritizing security, traders can trade with confidence and minimize the risks associated with automated trading.

Best Practices for Secure Coding Trading System

Secure coding practices are more important than ever, especially in the financial industry where trading systems handle sensitive and valuable information. The consequences of a security breach in a trading system can be catastrophic, leading to financial losses, reputational damage, and even legal liabilities. Therefore, it is crucial for developers working on trading systems to follow best practices for secure coding to ensure the integrity and confidentiality of the system.

Here are some best practices for secure coding in trading systems:

Input Validation: One of the most common vulnerabilities in trading systems is input validation. Developers should always validate and sanitize user input to prevent injection attacks such as SQL injection, cross-site scripting, and command injection. Input validation should be done on both the client and server side to ensure that only valid and safe data is accepted by the system.

Authentication and Authorization: Proper authentication and authorization mechanisms should be implemented to ensure that only authorized users have access to the trading system. Strong password policies, multi-factor authentication, and session management techniques should be used to prevent unauthorized access to the system.

Data Encryption: Sensitive data such as user credentials,

financial transactions, and market data should be encrypted both in transit and at rest. Secure protocols such as TLS should be used for communication between the client and server, and data should be encrypted using strong encryption algorithms to prevent unauthorized access.

Secure Coding Practices: Developers should follow secure coding practices such as input validation, output encoding, secure error handling, and secure configuration management. They should also avoid using insecure functions and libraries that are prone to security vulnerabilities.

Secure Communication: Trading systems often communicate with external systems such as market data providers, clearinghouses, and other trading platforms. Secure communication protocols such as HTTPS, SSH, and SFTP should be used to ensure the confidentiality and integrity of data exchanged between systems.

Secure Development Lifecycle: A secure development lifecycle should be followed to ensure that security is integrated into every phase of the software development process. This includes requirements analysis, design, coding, testing, deployment, and maintenance. Security testing techniques such as static analysis, dynamic analysis, and penetration testing should be used to identify and mitigate security vulnerabilities.

Secure Configuration Management: Proper configuration management practices should be followed to ensure that the trading system is configured securely. Default passwords, unnecessary services, and insecure configurations should be avoided to reduce the attack surface of the system.

Monitoring and Logging: Logging and monitoring mechanisms should be implemented to track and analyze security events in the trading system. Security logs should be regularly reviewed to detect and respond to security incidents in a timely manner.

Patch Management: Regular security updates and patches should be applied to the trading system to address known vulnerabilities and security issues. A patch management process should be in place to ensure that the system is up to date with the latest security patches.

Security Awareness Training: Developers, administrators, and users of the trading system should receive security awareness training to educate them about security best practices, common security threats, and how to respond to security incidents. Security training should be conducted regularly to keep the team informed about the latest security trends and threats.

Secure coding practices are essential for building secure and reliable trading systems in the financial industry. By following best practices for secure coding, developers can reduce the risk of security breaches and protect the integrity and confidentiality of the trading system.

It is important for organizations to invest in security measures and provide training to their employees to ensure that their trading systems are secure and resilient

172

against cyber threats. Remember, security is everyone's responsibility, and by following best practices for secure coding, we can create a safer and more secure trading environment for all stakeholders.

Handling API Keys and Sensitive Data with python - scripts

The use of Application Programming Interfaces (APIs) has become increasingly common. APIs allow different software applications to communicate with each other, enabling the exchange of data and functionality. However, when working with APIs, it is crucial to handle sensitive data such as API keys securely to prevent unauthorized access and potential security breaches.

We will discuss how to handle API keys and sensitive data securely using Python scripts. We will explore best practices for storing and managing API keys, as well as demonstrate how to access APIs while keeping sensitive data secure.

Storing API Keys Securely

One of the most important aspects of handling API keys securely is to store them in a secure location. Storing API keys directly in your code or in a publicly accessible file is a security risk, as they can be easily accessed by unauthorized individuals. Instead, it is recommended to store API keys in environment variables or configuration files that are not publicly accessible.

Environment variables are variables that are set outside of the code and are accessible to the operating system and the code running on it. By storing API keys in environment variables, you can prevent them from being exposed in your codebase. Here is an example of how you

174

can store an API key in an environment variable using Python:

```python
import os

# Set the API key as an environment variable
os.environ['API_KEY'] = 'your_api_key_here'

# Access the API key from the environment variable
api_key = os.environ.get('API_KEY')
```

By using environment variables to store API keys, you can keep them secure and prevent them from being exposed in your codebase. Additionally, you can easily change the API key without having to modify your code.

Another option for storing API keys securely is to use configuration files. Configuration files are files that contain settings and parameters for your application. By storing API keys in a configuration file, you can keep them separate from your codebase and prevent them from being exposed. Here is an example of how you can store an API key in a configuration file using Python:

```python
import configparser

# Create a configuration file
config = configparser.ConfigParser()
```

```python
config['API'] = {'api_key': 'your_api_key_here'}

# Write the configuration file
with open('config.ini', 'w') as configfile:
config.write(configfile)

# Read the API key from the configuration file config =
configparser.ConfigParser() config.read('config.ini')
api_key = config['API']['api_key']
```

By storing API keys in configuration files, you can keep them secure and separate from your codebase. You can also easily change the API key by modifying the configuration file.

Accessing APIs Securely

Once you have securely stored your API keys, you can access APIs using Python scripts while keeping sensitive data secure. When accessing APIs, it is important to use secure methods such as HTTPS to encrypt data transmission and prevent unauthorized access.

Here is an example of how you can access an API securely using Python:

```python
python import requests

# Set the API endpoint and parameters url =
'https://api.example.com/data'
params = {'api_key': api_key, 'param1': 'value1', 'param2': 'value2'}
```

```
# Make a GET request to the API endpoint response =
requests.get(url, params=params)

# Check if the request was successful if
response.status_code == 200:
data = response.json()print(data)
else:
print('Error: Unable to access API')
```

In this example, we are using the requests library in Python to make a GET request to an API endpoint. We are passing the API key as a parameter to authenticate the request. By using HTTPS and passing the API key securely, we can access the API while keeping sensitive data secure.

It is important to note that when accessing APIs, you should always follow the API provider's guidelines and best practices for authentication and data protection. Some APIs may require additional security measures such as Auth authentication or API tokens. By following the API provider's guidelines, you can ensure that your APIaccess is secure and compliant with their security requirements.

Chapter 16: Regulatory Considerations in Trading

Regulatory considerations play a crucial role in the trading industry. As the financial markets continue to evolve and become more complex, regulatory bodies are tasked with ensuring fair and transparent trading practices. In this chapter, we will explore the various regulatory considerations that traders need to be aware of when engaging in trading activities.

Regulatory Bodies

There are several regulatory bodies around the world that oversee trading activities in their respective jurisdictions. Some of the most prominent regulatory bodies include the Securities and Exchange Commission(SEC) in the United States, the Financial Conduct Authority (FCA) in the United Kingdom, and the European Securities and Markets Authority (ESMA) in the European Union.

These regulatory bodies are responsible for enforcing rules and regulations that are designed to protect investors and maintain the integrity of the financial markets. They have the authority to investigate and prosecute individuals and firms that engage in fraudulent or manipulative trading practices.

Compliance Requirements

Traders are required to comply with a wide range of regulations when engaging in trading activities. These regulations cover various aspects of trading, including market manipulation, insider trading, and disclosure requirements.

Market manipulation refers to the practice of artificially inflating or deflating the price of a security in order to profit from the price movement. This practice is illegal and can result in severe penalties for those found guilty of engaging in it.

Insider trading occurs when individuals trade on non-public information about a company that could impact the price of its securities. This practice is also illegal and can result in criminal charges and significant fines.

Disclosure requirements mandate that traders provide accurate and timely information about their trading activities to regulatory authorities. Failure to comply with these requirements can result in penalties and sanctions.

Risk Management

Regulatory bodies also require traders to implement robust risk management practices to protect themselves and their clients from potential losses. These practices include setting limits on trading positions, monitoring marketconditions, and implementing controls to prevent unauthorized trading activities.

Traders are also required to maintain adequate capital reserves to cover potential losses and ensure that they have sufficient liquidity to meet their obligations. Failure to maintain adequate capital reserves can result in regulatory sanctions and even the suspension of trading privileges.

Compliance Monitoring

Regulatory bodies conduct regular audits and inspections to ensure that traders are complying with regulations and operating in a transparent and ethical manner. These audits may include reviewing trading records, monitoring trading activities, and interviewing traders and other personnel.

Traders are required to cooperate fully with regulatory authorities during these audits and provide any information or documentation that is requested. Failure to cooperate can result in penalties and sanctions.

Enforcement Actions

Regulatory bodies have the authority to take enforcement actions against individuals and firms that violate trading regulations. These actions may include fines, suspensions, and even criminal charges in severe cases.

Traders who are found guilty of engaging in fraudulent or manipulative trading practices can face significant penalties, including monetary fines and the suspension or revocation of their trading licenses. In some cases, individuals may also face criminal charges and imprisonment.

Compliance with Trading Regulations

Compliance with trading regulations is a crucial aspect of any business that engages in trading activities. These regulations are put in place to ensure fair and transparent trading practices, protect investors, and maintain the integrity of financial markets. Failure to comply with trading regulations can result in severe consequences, including fines, legal action, and reputational damage. Therefore, it is essential for businesses to have robust compliance procedures in place to ensure they are meeting their regulatory obligations.

One of the key trading regulations that businesses must adhere to is the requirement to obtain the necessary licenses and permits to engage in trading activities. Depending on the nature of the trading activities, businesses may need to obtain licenses from regulatory authorities such as the Securities and Exchange Commission (SEC) or the Commodity Futures Trading Commission (CFTC). These licenses are typically granted after a thorough review of the business's operations and compliance with regulatory requirements. Failure to obtain the necessary licenses can result in the business being shut down or facing legal action.

In addition to obtaining the necessary licenses, businesses must also comply with regulations governing the conduct of trading activities. This includes rules around insider trading, market manipulation, and disclosure of material information.

Insider trading involves trading securities based on non-public information, which can give traders an unfair advantage over other market participants. Market manipulation involves artificially inflating or deflating the price of securities to profit from the resulting price movements. Disclosure of material informationrequires businesses to disclose any information that could have a material impact on the price of their securities.

Businesses must also comply with regulations around the handling of client funds and assets. This includes maintaining separate accounts for client funds, conducting regular audits of client assets, and ensuring that client assets are protected from misuse or theft. Failure to comply with these regulations can result in severe consequences, including the loss of client trust and legal action.

Another important aspect of compliance with trading regulations is the need to have robust internal controls and compliance procedures in place. This includes having clear policies and procedures for monitoring trading activities, conducting regular compliance training for staff, and implementing systems to detect and prevent potential violations of trading regulations. Businesses must also have mechanisms in place to report any suspected violations to regulatory authorities and take corrective action to address any issues that arise.

Compliance with trading regulations is not only a legal requirement but also a key component of maintaining a strong reputation in the market. Businesses that are seen to be operating in compliance with regulations are more likely to attract investors and customers who value transparency and integrity. Conversely, businesses that are found to be in violation of trading regulations can suffer significant reputational damage, which can impact their ability to attract and retain clients.

Compliance with trading regulations is a critical aspect of any business that engages in trading activities. Businesses must ensure they have the necessary licenses and permits to operate, comply with regulations governing trading activities, and have robust internal controls and compliance procedures in place.

Failure to comply with trading regulations can result in severe consequences, including fines, legal action, and reputational damage. Therefore, businesses must prioritize compliance with trading regulations to protect their interests and maintain the integrity of financial markets.

Implementing Compliance Checks in Trading

Implementing compliance checks in trading is a crucial aspect of ensuring that financial markets operate in a fair and transparent manner. Compliance checks are designed to prevent fraud, market manipulation, and other unethical practices that can undermine the integrity of the trading system. By implementing compliance checks, regulators can help protect investors and maintain confidence in the financial markets.

Compliance checks in trading involve a series of measures and procedures that are put in place to ensure that all participants in the market are following the rules and regulations that govern trading activities. These checks are designed to detect and prevent violations of securities laws, as well as to promote market integrity and investor protection. Compliance checks can take many forms, including pre-trade checks, post-trade checks, and ongoing monitoring of trading activities.

One of the key benefits of implementing compliance checks in trading is that they can help to detect and prevent market manipulation. Market manipulation is a serious concern in financial markets, as it can distort prices, mislead investors, and undermine the integrity of the market. By implementing compliance checks, regulators can help to identify and investigate suspicious trading activities that may be indicative of market manipulation. This can help to deter would-be manipulators and protect investors from potential harm.

Another benefit of implementing compliance checks in trading is that they can help to prevent insider trading. Insider trading occurs when individuals with access to non-public information about a company use that information to trade securities for their own benefit. Insider trading is illegal and can have serious consequences for both the individuals involved and the integrity of the financial markets. By implementing compliance checks, regulators can help to detect and prevent insider trading before it occurs, thereby protecting investors and maintaining confidence in the market.

Compliance checks in trading can also help to prevent other forms of fraud and misconduct. For example, compliance checks can help to detect and prevent front-running, which occurs when a trader places orders on behalf of a client before placing orders for their own account to take advantage of the price movement.
Compliance checks can also help to prevent wash trading, which occurs when a trader simultaneously buys andsells the same security to create the appearance of trading activity. By implementing compliance checks, regulators can help to detect and prevent these and other forms of fraud and misconduct, thereby promoting a fair and transparent trading environment.

In order to implement compliance checks in trading, regulators must have access to the necessary tools and resources. This may include access to trading data, surveillance systems, and other technology that can help to monitor trading activities and detect potential violations of securities laws. Regulators must also have the authority to enforce compliance checks and take action against individuals or firms that are found to be in violation of the rules.

In addition to regulatory oversight, market participants also play a key role in implementing compliance checks in trading. Firms that engage in trading activities must have their own compliance programs in place to ensure that they are following the rules and regulations that govern their activities.

This may include conducting regular audits, training employees on compliance issues, and implementing internal controls to prevent fraud and misconduct. By working together with regulators, market participants can help to promote a culture of compliance and ensure that the financial markets operate in a fair and transparent manner.

Overall, implementing compliance checks in trading is essential for maintaining the integrity of the financial markets and protecting investors from fraud and misconduct. By detecting and preventing violations of securities laws, compliance checks can help to promote market integrity and investor protection.

Regulators, market participants, and other stakeholders must work together to ensure that compliance checks are effectively implemented and enforced, thereby promoting a fair and transparent trading environment for all participants.

Chapter 17: Future of Automated Trading

Automated trading, also known as algorithmic trading, has revolutionized the financial markets in recent years. With the use of complex algorithms and computer programs, traders can execute trades at lightning speed and with precision that was previously unimaginable. In this chapter, we will explore the future of automated tradingand the trends that are shaping the industry.

One of the key trends in automated trading is the increasing use of artificial intelligence (AI) and machine learning. These technologies allow traders to analyze vast amounts of data and identify patterns that human traders may overlook. By using AI-powered algorithms, traders can make more informed decisions and executetrades with greater accuracy.

Another trend in automated trading is the rise of high-frequency trading (HFT). HFT firms use sophisticated algorithms to execute trades in milliseconds, taking advantage of small price discrepancies in the market. While HFT has been controversial due to concerns about market manipulation, it is likely to continue to play a significant role in the future of automated trading.

One of the challenges facing automated trading is the increasing complexity of financial markets. As markets become more interconnected and volatile, traders need to adapt their algorithms to changing conditions. This requires constant monitoring and updating of algorithms, which can be time-consuming and costly.

Regulation is another key issue for the future of automated trading. Regulators are increasingly concerned about the risks posed by automated trading, such as market manipulation and systemic risk. As a result, there may be stricter regulations imposed on automated trading in the future, which could impact the profitability of firms that rely on these technologies.

Despite these challenges, the future of automated trading looks bright. As technology continues to advance, traders will have access to more powerful algorithms and data analysis tools. This will enable them to make better trading decisions and adapt to changing market conditions more effectively.

One of the key benefits of automated trading is its ability to remove human emotions from the trading process. Emotions such as fear and greed can cloud judgment and lead to poor decision-making. By using algorithms to execute trades, traders can avoid these emotional pitfalls and stick to their trading strategies more consistently.

Another benefit of automated trading is its ability to execute trades at high speeds. In today's fast-paced markets, speed is crucial to capturing profitable trading opportunities. Automated trading allows traders to execute trades in milliseconds, giving them a competitive edge over human traders.

In conclusion, the future of automated trading looks

promising. With the use of AI, machine learning, and high-frequency trading, traders can make more informed decisions and execute trades with greater speed and accuracy. While there are challenges such as market complexity and regulation, the benefits of automated trading far outweigh the risks. As technology continues to advance, we can expect to see even greater innovations in the field of automated trading in the years to come.

Emerging Trends and Technologies Trading

Trading has come a long way from the days of shouting orders on the trading floor to the use of sophisticated algorithms and artificial intelligence. With the advancement of technology, the trading landscape has been rapidly evolving, and new trends and technologies are constantly emerging to improve efficiency, accuracy, and speed in trading. In this article, we will explore some of the emerging trends and technologies in trading that are shaping the future of the industry.

Artificial Intelligence and Machine Learning

One of the most significant trends in trading is the use of artificial intelligence (AI) and machine learning. These technologies have revolutionized trading by enabling traders to analyze vast amounts of data in real-time and make informed decisions.

AI and machine learning algorithms can quickly identify patterns and trends in the market, predict market movements, and execute trades at lightning speed. This has made trading more efficient and profitable for traders, as they can make better-informed decisions based on data-driven insights.

Blockchain Technology

Blockchain technology is another emerging trend in trading that is transforming the way transactions are conducted. Blockchain is a decentralized and secure digital ledger that records transactions across a network of computers. This technology ensures transparency, security, and immutability of transactions, making it ideal for trading. Blockchain technology is being used in trading to streamline settlement processes, reduce transaction costs, and eliminate the need for intermediaries. With blockchain, traders can execute trades faster, securely, and at lower costs, leading to increased efficiency and profitability.

High-Frequency Trading

High-frequency trading (HFT) is a trading strategy that uses powerful computers and algorithms to execute a large number of trades in milliseconds. HFT has become a popular trend in trading due to its ability to capitalize on small price movements and generate profits quickly.

Traders use HFT to take advantage of arbitrage opportunities, exploit market inefficiencies, and execute trades at lightning speed. However, HFT has also raised concerns about market manipulation and instability, leading regulators to impose stricter regulations on this trading strategy.

Robo-Advisors

Robo-advisors are automated trading platforms that use algorithms to manage investment portfolios on behalf of clients. These platforms offer personalized investment advice, asset allocation, and portfolio rebalancing based on an individual's risk tolerance and financial goals. Robo-advisors have gained popularity in trading due to their low fees, accessibility, and convenience. Traders can use robo-advisors to automate their investment decisions, reduce human error, and achieve better investment returns. With the rise of robo-advisors, traditional financial advisors are facing stiff competition and are forced to adapt to the changing landscape of trading.

Quantum Computing

Quantum computing is a cutting-edge technology that has the potential to revolutionize trading by solving complex mathematical problems at an unprecedented speed. Quantum computers can process vast amounts of data simultaneously and perform calculations that are impossible for classical computers.

In trading, quantum computing can be used to optimize trading strategies, analyze market data in real-time, and predict market trends with higher accuracy. While quantum computing is still in its early stages, it holds great promise for the future of trading and is expected to disrupt the industry in the coming years.

Internet of Things (IoT)

The Internet of Things (IoT) is a network of interconnected devices that communicate and exchange data with each other over the internet. IoT technology is being used in trading to collect real-time market data, monitor trading activities, and automate trading processes.

Traders can use IoT devices to track market trends, analyze trading patterns, and execute trades based on predefined criteria. IoT technology has made trading more efficient, transparent, and responsive to market changes, leading to better decision-making and improved tradingoutcomes.

Big Data Analytics

Big data analytics is a powerful technology that enables traders to analyze large volumes of data to extract valuable insights and make informed decisions. Traders use big data analytics to identify market trends, analyze trading patterns, and predict market movements with greater accuracy.

By leveraging big data analytics, traders can gain a competitive edge in trading by making data-driven decisions, optimizing trading strategies, and maximizing profits. Big data analytics is becoming increasingly important in trading as the volume and complexity of data continue to grow, making it essential for traders to harness the power of data analytics to stay ahead of the competition.

Cloud Computing
Cloud computing is a technology that allows traders to access trading platforms, data, and resources over the internet without the need for physical infrastructure. Cloud computing offers scalability, flexibility, and cost-effectiveness, making it ideal for traders who want to access trading tools and resources on-demand. Traders can use cloud computing to execute trades, analyze market

data, and collaborate with other traders in real-time.
Cloud computing has made trading more accessible, efficient, and secure, enabling traders to trade from anywhere at any time with ease.

Preparing for the Future in Trading System

Trading has been an integral part of human civilization for centuries. From the barter system to the modern stock market, trading has evolved significantly over time. With the advancement of technology, trading systems have become more efficient and accessible to a larger audience. However, the future of trading systems is constantly evolving, and traders need to adapt to stay ahead of the curve.

Preparing for the future in trading systems requires a deep understanding of market trends, technological advancements, and regulatory changes. Traders must constantly educate themselves and stay updated on the latest developments in the industry to make informed decisions and maximize their profits. In this article, we will discuss some key strategies for preparing for the future in trading systems.

One of the most important aspects of preparing for the future in trading systems is staying informed about market trends. The global economy is constantly changing, and traders need to be aware of the factors that can impact their investments. This includes keeping track of economic indicators, geopolitical events, and industry news that can affect the market. By staying informed, traders can make better decisions and adjust their strategies accordingly.

Another key aspect of preparing for the future in trading systems is understanding technological advancements. The trading industry is constantly evolving, with new

195

technologies being developed to improve efficiency and accuracy. Traders need to stay updated on the latest trading platforms, algorithms, and tools that can help them make better decisions and execute trades more effectively. By embracing technology, traders can gain a competitive edge in the market and stay ahead of the curve.

In addition to market trends and technological advancements, traders also need to be aware of regulatory changes that can impact their trading activities. Governments around the world are constantly updating regulations to protect investors and ensure the stability of the financial markets.

Traders need to stay informed about these changes and comply with all relevant regulations to avoid legal issues and financial penalties. By staying compliant, traders can build trust with their clients and protect their investments in the long run.

In order to prepare for the future in trading systems, traders also need to develop a solid risk management strategy. Trading is inherently risky, and traders need to be prepared for unexpected events that can impact their investments. By diversifying their portfolios, setting stop-loss orders, and using risk management tools, traders can minimize their losses and protect their capital. It is also important for traders to have a clear exit strategy in place to limit their losses and maximize their profits.

Furthermore, traders need to constantly educate themselves and improve their skills to stay competitive in the market. The trading industry is highly competitive, and traders need to constantly adapt to new trends and technologies to stay ahead of the curve. By attending workshops, seminars, and online courses, traders can enhance their knowledge and skills and improve their trading performance. Continuous learning is essential for success in the trading industry, and traders need to invest in their education to stay relevant in the market.

Preparing for the future in trading systems requires a combination of market knowledge, technological expertise, regulatory compliance, risk management, and continuous education.

Traders need to stay informed about market trends, embrace technology, comply with regulations, manage their risks, and improve their skills to succeed in the competitive trading industry. By following these strategies, traders can prepare for the future and maximize their profits in the ever-changing trading landscape.

Conclusion

As we reach the end of ***Python for Automated Trading Systems: Building Your Own Bots for Stock and Crypto Markets***, it's time to reflect on the journey we've embarked upon together. We've navigated through the intricate world of automated trading, unlocking the potential of Python to create sophisticated, efficient, and profitable trading systems.

From the foundational understanding of the financial markets and the role of automation, to diving deep into the technicalities of Python programming, we've built a robust framework for developing your own trading bots. We've explored data analysis, backtesting strategies, integrating APIs, and implementing machine learning algorithms to predict market movements with remarkable accuracy. Each chapter has been designed to equip you with the skills and knowledge necessary to thrive in the fast-paced, ever-evolving world of stock and cryptocurrency trading.

The main takeaway from this book is clear: with the power of Python, you can transform the way you approach trading. Automation is not just a tool; it's a game-changer. By leveraging automated trading systems, you can execute trades with precision, eliminate emotional biases, and capitalize on market opportunities around the clock. Whether you're targeting the stock market or the dynamic crypto space, the principles and techniques covered in this book provide a comprehensive roadmap to success.

Creating automated trading systems is not just about writing code; it's about crafting a strategy that aligns with your financial goals, risk tolerance, and market insights. It's about continuously refining your approach, learning from your successes and setbacks, and staying ahead of the curve in an industry that never stands still.

As you continue your journey beyond this book, remember that the world of automated trading is vast and full of opportunities. Keep experimenting, keep learning, and most importantly, keep pushing the boundaries of what's possible. The skills you've acquired here are not just tools for today but are building blocks for a future where technology and finance intertwine even more seamlessly.

In conclusion, your journey in mastering automated trading with Python has just begun. The insights, techniques, and strategies you've learned will serve as your compass in navigating the complex and exciting markets ahead. Embrace the power of automation, harness the capabilities of Python, and let your trading bots lead you to new heights of financial success.

Biography

J.P. Morgan is a seasoned expert in the field of finance and technology, with a deep-rooted passion for automated trading systems. With years of experience in the dynamic worlds of stock and cryptocurrency markets, J.P. Morgan has dedicated his career to developing cutting-edge trading bots that leverage the power of Python to achieve consistent profitability.

J.P. Morgan's journey into the realm of automated trading began with a fascination for the intersection of technology and finance. Armed with a strong background in programming and a keen interest in investment strategies, he has continuously pushed the boundaries of what's possible in the trading industry. His expertise in Python and its application in creating sophisticated trading algorithms has made him a sought-after authority in the field.

Beyond his professional pursuits, J.P. Morgan is an enthusiastic advocate for continuous learning and innovation. He spends his free time experimenting with new trading strategies, analyzing market trends, and staying ahead of the latest developments in the crypto space. His personal interests include delving into the intricacies of financial markets, exploring advancements in automated systems, and sharing his knowledge with aspiring traders and developers.

When he's not immersed in the world of finance and technology, J.P. Morgan enjoys building and tinkering with new projects, always seeking ways to enhance efficiency and performance. His enthusiasm for the subject matter is infectious, and he is dedicated to empowering others to harness the potential of automated trading.

With *Python for Automated Trading Systems: Building Your Own Bots for Stock and Crypto Markets*, J.P. Morgan brings his wealth of knowledge and experience to the forefront, offering readers an engaging and comprehensive guide to mastering the art of automated trading. His commitment to excellence and passion for the subject shine through every page, making this book an invaluable resource for anyone looking to thrive in the fast-paced world of automated trading.

Glossary: Python for automated trading systems

Algorithmic Trading: Algorithmic trading is a method of trading that uses computer algorithms to automatically execute trades based on predefined criteria. These algorithms can analyze market data, identify trading opportunities, and execute trades at high speeds.

API (Application Programming Interface): An API is a set of rules and protocols that allow different software applications to communicate with each other. In the context of automated trading systems, APIs are used to connect trading platforms to external data sources, such as market data feeds.

Backtesting: Backtesting is the process of testing a trading strategy using historical market data to evaluate its performance. This allows traders to assess the effectiveness of their strategies before risking real capital.

Broker API: A broker API is an API provided by a brokerage firm that allows traders to connect their automated trading systems to the broker's trading platform. This enables traders to execute trades directly through the broker's platform.

Candlestick Chart: A candlestick chart is a type of financial chart used to represent price movements in a particular time period. Each candlestick represents the opening, closing, high, and low prices for that period.

Data Analysis: Data analysis is the process of examining, cleaning, and transforming data to extract useful information. In the context of automated trading systems, data analysis is used to identify trading opportunitiesand make informed trading decisions.

Execution Strategy: An execution strategy is a set of rules and parameters that determine how trades are executed in an automated trading system. This includes factors such as order size, order type, and timing oftrades.

Financial Data: Financial data refers to data related to financial markets, such as stock prices, trading volumes, and economic indicators. This data is used by automated trading systems to analyze market conditions and make trading decisions.

Machine Learning: Machine learning is a branch of artificial intelligence that focuses on developing algorithms that can learn from and make predictions based on data. In the context of automated trading systems, machine learning algorithms can be used to analyze market data and identify trading patterns.

Market Data Feed: A market data feed is a stream of real-time data that provides information on market prices, trading volumes, and other market-related information. Automated trading systems rely on market data feeds to make trading decisions.

Order Management System: An order management system

is a software application used by traders to manage and track their orders. In the context of automated trading systems, order management systems are used to submit, monitor, and track trades.

Python: Python is a high-level programming language that is widely used in the development of automated trading systems. Its simplicity and readability make it an ideal choice for traders who want to build their own trading algorithms.

Quantitative Analysis: Quantitative analysis is a method of analyzing financial markets using mathematical and statistical models. In the context of automated trading systems, quantitative analysis is used to develop trading strategies based on historical market data.

Risk Management: Risk management is the process of identifying, assessing, and mitigating risks in trading. In the context of automated trading systems, risk management strategies are used to minimize the impact of losses and protect capital.

Technical Indicators: Technical indicators are mathematical calculations based on historical market data that are used to analyze market trends and predict future price movements. Automated trading systems often use technical indicators to make trading decisions.

Trading Algorithm: A trading algorithm is a set of rules and instructions that define how trades are executed in an automated trading system. These algorithms can be simple or complex, depending on the trading strategy being implemented.

Trading Platform: A trading platform is a software application that allows traders to execute trades and monitor market data. In the context of automated trading systems, trading platforms are used to connect to broker APIs and execute trades automatically.

Volatility: Volatility is a measure of the degree of variation in the price of a financial instrument over time. High volatility indicates large price swings, while low volatility indicates smaller price movements. Automated trading systems often adjust their trading strategies based on market volatility.